I0623405

The Deep End of the Pool
Where you swim, tread water, struggle, or drown.

Dave Edwards

Copyright © 2024 Dave Edwards

All rights reserved. No part of this book may be reproduced or transmitted in any form or by any means, electronic or mechanical, including photocopying, recording or by any information storage and retrieval system without permission in writing from the publisher.

MuseInks Press—Coloma, MI
ISBN: 979-8-9906828-0-1
Library of Congress Control Number: 2024911954
Title: *The Deep End of the Pool: Where you swim, tread water, struggle, or drown.*
Author: Dave Edwards
Digital distribution | 2024
Paperback | 2024

Published in the United States by New Book Authors Publishing

Dedication

I dedicate this book to Mom and Dad. Eddy and Stella. I am grateful for their belief in their children and the gentle nudge to see the world, not as we saw it, but as a place where we could and should aspire to achieve something greater than we imagined, a place where we were to ply our talents, whatever they may be, moving always forward, without fear.

Table of Contents

Chapter 1
The beginning

This was déjà vu all over again.

Each year since junior high, sixteen-year-old Everett "Eddy" Edwards had Miss Cline for a teacher. It wasn't always the same Miss Cline, but to him they felt interchangeable. Though Eddy was well spoken and well read, with a very rounded world view, his beliefs and demeanor were hardly mainstream.

It was 1943. In the outside world, World War II raged. The United States had entered the war over a year ago after the Japanese attack on Pearl Harbor. Many students were already feeling the strain, with brothers, uncles, friends, and other family members being called to arms to fight in a distant land.

Eddy was a junior at Hinsdale High school just outside Chicago, Illinois. As he sat at lunch, reviewing his grades, he couldn't escape the feeling that he was once again facing an arch enemy: one of the Cline sisters.

"How can it be that no matter what type of work I put in, I can't get anything but some sort of middling grade from a Cline sister? Good work, bad work, it's no difference."

Eddy turned to his friend Webb. "Have you seen any difference in your grades from Miss Cline?"

Webb and Eddy had been friends for what seemed like forever—ever since grade school.

Webb's response echoed Eddy suspicion. "I think these grades are last year's grades." In the throes of righteous indignation, Eddy decided to run a comparison.

"Has anyone's grades from Miss Cline changed at all from last year to this?" he asked.

Of the small group at his table, everyone was in agreement.

Nope, haven't seen any grade change at all. In fact, it's exactly the same as last year.

To Eddy, this felt like a full flung conspiracy. He ran a quick poll and checked with other friends, asking around to see if anyone else was having the same experience. Everyone was.

Over the next several weeks, Eddy and his friends branched out, trying to get a sizable sampling of classmates who had one of the Cline sisters for a teacher. In general, the overall conclusion from their poll was that, depending on where a student first notched into the grade hierarchy, their grade point was set. It was never going to change.

Armed with this information, Eddy set about righting the wrong. His plan to blow open the plot to deprive them of proper grading was quite simple, though it required a few of the students to put themselves on the line. Eddy was one of the first to volunteer. With a couple of others in tow, and a full supporting cast, they were set.

For the next marking period, Eddy and his friends would do absolutely nothing in Miss Cline's class. No participation, no homework, no reading or studying of the materials. They would do the type of work that deserves a failing grade.

The next phase required a bit of help, but they had plenty of volunteers. The following marking period, these same students needed to be coached to become experts in all class-related matters that came before them. They read their material, studied the material, and got their friends to quiz them so they could pass any test put in front of them without blinking an eye. The "slackers" did straight A work.

While Eddy was a good student, he was not normally an A student. He took his grades seriously, but was never the straight A scholar his older sister Dorothy was.

The whole ruse took months to unfold, they were determined to get to the truth.

The first six weeks, Eddy and two friends executed the first phase of their plan. They must have felt a certain joy in just tanking the class, participating in a joke that only a few were in on. At the end of the grading period, all felt "mission accomplished." Convinced they had put in failing work, they waited for their grades to be posted.

For all three, the grades were exactly the same as they had been the previous marking period. Eddy wasn't sure if it was more of an "ah-ha" moment or if he was relieved that he didn't have to explain to his parents why he had flunked a class.

The next six weeks were more daunting for the trio of grade warriors. There was a ton of extra work to do. If Eddy and his friends didn't understand something, they studied until it was clear. Their classmates watched, fascinated at what they were trying to pull off, and their willingness to completely fail the previous grading period. Now, they were turning in what was arguably their best work ever, putting all that they had into their classwork.

What better cause, they reasoned, than to bring down a teacher they didn't much like?

After another six weeks, and with so much extra work behind them, the whole class waited for grades to come out. This time, Eddy and his friends didn't fear failure. They reveled in a sense of accomplishment at finishing something and having done so at a much higher level than anything they'd done before. Even though they knew their grade theory, a part of them half expected to see a reward for all their extra effort.

In the end, the grades were released: exactly the same as their grades the previous marking period. No change at all. Their theory, their test, their belief that they were being wronged had all proven true. Still, with all their extra work, it was a bitter pill to swallow.

Eddy took comfort in knowing that they would, no doubt, be rewarded when the whole scam was revealed for all to see.

Eddy and his cohorts now had proof of Miss Cline's shortcomings. They had saved all their paperwork. They put together all of their grades, along with an outline of their original theory and test. Armed with this information, they approached the administration.

Principal Mossman was the head of the administration food chain. Mossman, in his second year as high school principal at Hinsdale, had already butted heads with the student body. He encouraged no discussion. Instead, he would ignore and patronize. He clearly considered himself a big fish in a little pond. Why listen to a bunch of kids who were barely treading water in the shallow end of the pool? Mossman's controlling approach to students who would, very shortly, be asked to go fight for their country treated them as children and was insulting— resulting in what Eddy described as a "general uneasiness" throughout the school.

Eddy was aware of the way the students felt about Mossman, but with proof of the unfair grading process in hand, he and his band of co-conspirators made their way to the high school office. With self-assured bravado, they presented their case.

Principal Mossman looked them over. How dare a bunch of children tell him how to run his school? He glanced at the evidence they provided and then told Eddy and his crew, "it's none of your business. Get back to class."

Furious, Eddy obeyed. But he vowed this would not be the end of the story.

Chapter 2
The start of Circle Pines

In 1938, when Eddy was 12, the Edwards family became involved with the formation of a new summer camp in Michigan. Eddy and his brother Bruce had been attending a YMCA camp in Wisconsin, but this was different. This involvement not only shaped young Eddy in his school years but also formed a foundation for the rest of his life.

In 1937, the Ashland Folk School of Grant, Michigan, an outgrowth of the Danish folk school movement that began in 1882, had outgrown its Ashland facility and was looking for a new home.

Some said that the reason to move was because the State Fire Marshal had condemned the building which was home to the school. Another rumor held that the decision to condemn the building was due in part to local political pressure and how some people felt about the progressive activities taking place at Ashland. For some, the folk school was seen to be aligned with the Cooperative movement, the Farmer's Union, and the League for Independent Political Action.

Friends of Ashland learned that Chief Noonday Camp, a soon-to-be completed Civilian Conservation Corps' camp in Barry County, MI, about a 60-mile trip from Grant, was available to rent. The folk school decided to rent the facility for their summer school. When the members of the school board got together in April of 1938 to sign the lease, Chester Graham, the director of the Ashland Folk School, found that he had lost control of his board and the lease was signed by The Central States Cooperative League. The Co-op took over the management of the summer school and rental and the Ashland summer school changed its name to Circle Pines Center.

Chief Noonday Conservation Camp was named for Chief Noonday or, more correctly, Noahquageshik, a Chief of the Grand River band of Ottawa Native Americans in what became the state of Michigan. The facility had newly completed a cluster of rustic buildings in a wooded natural setting near Mud Lake in an area now known as Yankee Springs Recreation Area.

The buildings were in the same style as those in our state and national parks. The small cabin accommodated up to 10 people on bunk beds with little, if any, other furniture. A centrally located dining- and meeting-hall was built with wide plank and batten siding and generous use of local stone for foundations and fireplaces. The color of choice was almost always dark brown.[*]

The Conservation Corps camps that went up throughout the United States were constructed through the Forest Service, which had a stable of architects who designed buildings based on a very utilitarian platform, trying as best they could to utilize as many local natural materials in the construction, often working on a shoestring budget. They also tried to adapt the architecture to the location of the building. That's why in the more western states there is a wide range of styles, from the log cabin style used in the mountain regions to the pueblo styles used in the southwest desert areas.

Camp Chief Noonday became the new home for the newly formed Circle Pines Center. Circle Pines arranged to rent the facility for the summer of 1939 while building a program for families based on cooperation. They had a plan to explore the different aspects of the cooperative movement, including recreation, medicine, education, finance, housing, and the relationship between managers and employees. They also looked at the relationship between producers and consumers. Their new director, Dr. David Sonquist, a sociologist, had

---

[*] *Part of the reason for the dark brown color was the use of cheap, readily available and more water-resistant creosote-based finishes.*

written several books on cooperation as a way of life.

As members of the Central States cooperative, the Edwards family joined other families in embracing Circle Pines. Whole programs were geared toward children and young adults and there were also workshops and programs for the adults. In the spirit of cooperation, when there was work to be done, all were drawn in to help to benefit the whole. Eddy's older sister Dorothy became a cabin counselor.

Circle Pines was a lengthy drive from Hinsdale, on two lane state roads going from town to town. It was a good four- to five-hour trip, depending on weather, farm traffic, and the occasional break for fuel and food. Eddy's mother, Viola, always packed a picnic basket full of crackers, cheese, and seasoned meats along with healthy drinks for the journey.

Eddy had started out in the shallow end of the pool, but was now an avid swimmer, having already earned swimmer patches from his sessions during previous summers at Camp Edwards, in Wisconsin. Now, there was a new lake for him to explore.

He was prone to volunteer for any project that came along. He embraced new challenges and loved learning and doing new things. But when dinner came, the different groups gathered together for their evening meal, after which they often engaged in folk dancing and discussions on relevant topics of the day. This was totally different from Eddy's time at Camp Edwards.

This exposure to discussions influenced Eddy a great deal. He soaked up the healthy exchange of ideas, watching the adults work together and then talk about topics such as cooperation and racial harmony and trying to build a better world for all. Eddy was not alone. There were other young people, children his own age, with whom he would later talk about what the adults were discussing. Some of these "camp" friends also became his city friends. After summer passed, he connected with several of these camp friends when he returned to Hinsdale.

The camp's folk style recreation had an enormous influence on Eddy. Singing and dancing were at the forefront of Circle Pines' recreational activities, a carryover from the days of the Ashland Folk school. The previous director, Chester Graham, had simply stated, "The best way to get a cooperative state of mind was out of an hour of folk dancing."

Eddy loved music in all forms and the act of group singing and dancing deeply touched his spirit and soul. According to him, "he danced the dance of many lands." He joined the group singing and eventually became a song leader.

Folk songs—true Americana songs brought from the immigrant population both from their home countries and their new home—were a starting point. Such songs told the stories and memorialized the experiences of the writer. With accompaniment from both piano and guitar, everyone at camp was encouraged to join in.

This really sounds easier than it was. These were not the popular songs of the day, but ones which would need to be taught to the group and sung in styles with themes that may have been foreign to the different age groups. It was much the same with square dancing or folk dances from different cultures. It was a great physical way to blow off steam at the end of a long day.

Eddy not only embraced it; he lived it. People often found him singing and dancing his way through his daily routine.

Chapter 3
Eddy's first taste of junior high

B y the end of summer and into the fall of 1939, the world was in turmoil. On September 1, 1939, Germany invaded Poland. Propagandists from Germany claimed that Poland was persecuting ethnic Germans who lived in Poland. They also accused Poland's allies, Great Britain and France, of encircling Germany with plans to dismember it.

On September 2, Britain issued Germany an ultimatum: either leave Poland or Great

Britain would declare war against Germany.

The United States declared itself neutral.

Less than two weeks later, Russia invaded Poland, claiming they needed to come to the aid of their "blood brothers," the Ukrainians and Byelorussians whose land was trapped and illegally annexed by Poland.

September 1939 also brought with it the first day of school. Thirteen-year-old Everett Edwards entered Hinsdale junior high school, starting the eighth grade. The school was only six blocks from home, a relatively short walk.[*] In previous years, Eddy had attended Monroe grade school, the same distance away as the Junior high, only in a different direction.

The village of Hinsdale was a small, conservative, mostly Anglo, Christian suburb of Chicago in an area that, like most suburbs, had started out rural and slowly grown into small cities. The term "village" usually refers to a type of local government and legal status the area adopted. The suburbs

---

[*] *Probably uphill both ways.*

would rub one against another without the vast open farmlands that the mostly rural areas enjoyed, but as their population grew, many stayed with the simple form of local government with which they started.

Hinsdale had merged several of the smaller grade schools into one larger school. The high school district had expanded during the Depression to include Clarendon Hills and Westmont. It then further expanded to include Garfield and Madison schools.

The school building was like almost any suburban school of the day. Buildings relied on brick and block; the un-glazed bricks were painted with high gloss enamel. The floors were either some sort of painted concrete, terrazzo, or tile. The gymnasium was the only place with wood floors. With the number of people going through a school, the coldness of the décor helped keep the facility clean. A large part of the construction also leaned towards fire safety. Brick and block do not burn.

In 1867, the Hinsdale school system had the "Stone Building," as it was called, which was used as its schoolhouse. This multi-story building had a natural stone exterior. Interior framing of this style building was usually done with lathe and plaster over a wood frame, wood floor framing, and wood floors. In 1893, the building was at a total loss due to a fire. Classes were parsed out to churches and meeting halls in the village until new accommodation could be acquired.

Eddy found the classes in Junior high to be much more difficult and challenging than classes of previous years, but he also found them to be more engaging. His studies included core subjects of math, English, science, history, and social studies.

It was during his history and social studies class that he had his first encounter with one of the Cline sisters. He took an almost immediate dislike to her as a teacher, for when a student got a grade from Miss Cline, it was etched in stone, never changing.

"Once you get a grade from Miss Cline," he would say, "you have it for life."

Eddy's father, Everett Sr., was a self-made draftsman and mechanical engineer. He spent his free time designing houses, toys, and anything that struck his fancy. He designed the family home and did a good part of the construction himself. He acted as his own general contractor, providing specifications for bids, reviewing the bids, and hiring his own sub-contractors.

Everett Sr. was a quiet man, a pacifist who had deeply seated convictions. Both Everett and Eddy's mother, Viola, were very civic minded. Both were active with the national cooperative movement, which formed and became active worldwide with a joint mission of providing buying power for the general population. It gained steam in the United States after the passage of the Rural Electrification act of 1938, bringing electricity to all parts of rural America.

Early on, meetings were held in the Midwest at schools, camps, and other meeting facilities big enough to host large numbers of people. Everett Sr. and Viola actively participated with the Co-ops, believing in their mission. In addition to the National Co-op, Viola was active with the more politically aimed organization, the American Friends Service Committee, a Quaker organization whose mission was to help those who oppose war and those who were displaced by war, along with many other social issues such as women's rights and racial injustice.

Viola was always off to committee meetings of one type or another. She was adamant in her views and wasn't shy about letting anyone know what they were. She believed in a totally non-violent world. She vehemently opposed guns and wars for whatever reason.*

---

* *Viola had many strong views. A total teetotaler, she always claimed it was an alcoholic uncle who turned her away from all alcoholic beverages.*

Viola believed that if a person were going to do anything or participate in something, there had to be an educational payoff. She believed in questioning, "Am I learning? What was the purpose of my endeavor?"

As the school year progressed, there was much discussion throughout the country whether the United States should be involved in the current war or any war. Through the early stages of the conflict, the public was split between taking action or avoiding war at all costs.

There was no way to know how the invasion of Poland would expand to become what we now know as World War II. At home, Eddy was surrounded by pacifist political positions, like the many other Americans who were not in favor of the U.S. joining any type of war effort.

The Edwards Family attended the Union Church of Hinsdale and were active with all of the church offerings and activities. Eddy had perfect attendance at church and in Sunday school and saw himself as a devout Christian. Everyone in the family was civic minded, so it came as no surprise that Eddy, the youngest, would join and work with the various church youth clubs and with the Church Missionary Action Committee.

Eddy, like his father, saw himself as a quiet pacifist. He was not always vocal about his religious beliefs, but when asked would respond with the teaching of Jesus and how those teachings related to his positions on current events. Often, he would use those arguments to reinforce his position. But with the world view quickly shifting and changing toward the situation in Europe, he found more conflict in his pacifist stance.

Eddy gravitated toward the arts. He liked drawing and making things. He had started drum lessons at the age of 7 and enjoyed music and dance. There was a big upright piano at home to play on or play with. Dorothy had taken piano lessons and his brother Bruce, two years his senior, had studied violin.

Eddy explored sports as well. He enjoyed being active, especially if it meant getting outside. By 1939, in addition to being an avid swimmer, he played intramural football and went out for cheerleading, earning letters in both. He also tried tumbling, but hurt his back while doing a movement, creating a lifelong fear of going over backwards.

Chapter 4
Selective service act of 1940 and the draft

On September 16, 1940, Congress enacted the Selective Service act of 1940. After many months of discussions and political battles, by a house vote of 263-149 and a senate vote of 58-31, the United States was facing the first peacetime conscription, forever known as the draft.

The draft was to be held by a national lottery. If a young man were drafted, he was to serve 12 months of active duty, and then serve as a reserve for 10 years or until he reached 45 years of age. The Act provided that not more than 900,000 men were to be in training at any one time. The United States was not yet committed to war, but though it was a peacetime draft, everyone knew it was in preparation in case the United States entered the war.

This was not the first draft. Conscription had been used during several other conflicts throughout American history.

During the Civil War, a conscript could hire someone to serve in his place. Sometimes families would pool their resources and decide who they felt would be best to serve. The Army didn't seem to care as long as they had bodies willing to fill the positions. But the public was not all in favor of supporting a draft. There was much draft evasion and resistance. The vast majority of the population could not afford to hire someone or to gift another family for someone to replace their son in the service. While today we like to view service in the armed forces as honorable, in New York in 1863, there were draft wars to protest and avoid serving in the Army.

During World War I, the draft was enacted to provide for the main source of manpower for the war. In 1917, at the start of WWI, the U.S. had an armed force of less than 100,000 men.

At first, President Wilson hoped to only have a volunteer army, but it became clear that would not be a workable option. Wilson asked that the army increase to one million men, but six weeks after war was declared, only 73,000 had volunteered for service. Wilson accepted the recommendation of Secretary of War, Newton D. Baker, to institute a draft.

From the guidelines of the draft, men aged between 21 to 30 were required to register, but the age range was moved to 18 - 45. By the end of the War to end all Wars, 4.8 million men had served in the armed forces; over half had been drafted. Fewer than 350,000 had been considered as dodging the draft. One of the big changes from the draft during the Civil War was that no substitutes were allowed.

From section Three of the Selective Service Act of 1917.
No person liable to military service shall hereafter be permitted or allowed to furnish a substitute for such service; nor shall any substitute be received, enlisted, or enrolled in the military service of the United States; and no such person shall be permitted to escape such service or to be discharged therefrom prior to the expiration or his term of service by the payment of money or any other valuable thing whatsoever as consideration for release from military service or liability there to.

The Selective Service Act of 1917 allowed for classifications. A classification was to provide for a more selective way of choosing draftees.

Class 1 was deemed eligible and liable for military service. It included unmarried registrants with no dependents and married registrants with an independent spouse or one or more dependent children over 16 with sufficient income.

The other classes were either deferred or exempt.

There was more drafting by social class. Part of the logic was that if a soldier came from a poorer class, his work at home was likely to not be as important to the war effort. Agricultural labor and industrial labor were considered essential to the war effort, so were temporarily exempted. These workers, along with local officials, were all grouped into Class 3.

There was a protest about African Americans being drafted. Nevertheless, the war department included everyone in the draft. The vast majority of Black soldiers were put in labor functions, such as road building and freight hauling. Only two Black combat units were established during the war. Black Americans were entirely excluded from the Marine Corps and were consigned to menial labor in the Navy for the duration of the conflict.

There were challenges to the draft. In 1917, Emma Goldman challenged the draft law in federal court claiming it violated the Thirteenth Amendment and lost. Several others also challenged the draft, but all efforts were unsuccessful.

The draft allowed for conscientious objectors, but only for members of the "peace churches": the Amish, Mennonites, Quakers, and Moravian Brethren. All others were required to participate.

The armistice for WWI was signed on November 11, 1918, and by March 31, 1919, all local, district, and medical advisor boards were closed. By May, all Selective Service activities were terminated. It wasn't till the early days of WWII that the United States re-visited the draft.

With war raging in Europe, the United States started its first peacetime conscription. After the United States entered the war, the age was moved, requiring the registering of all men aged 18 to 65. In the summer of 1941, an amendment extended the required service from 12 months to 30 months, plus any additional time deemed necessary. The amendment passed by one vote.

The Selective Service Act of 1940 to provide for most circumstances of possible draftee created a variety of different classifications. By the war's end and the abolishment of the

Draft Act of 1940, there had been a total of 68 different classifications, but many lasted for only a short period, as there was an attempt to tweak the Act into the most workable form possible.

While the 1-A classification was the most common, there was a 1-A-O for non-combatant military service, or "conscientious objectors." Though many objectors told of a willingness to serve as long as they could serve without a combat role, there seemed to be a reluctance on the part of the local draft boards to grant this designation. This pushed for an objector to need to qualify for a 4-E classification and become a full Conscientious Objector assigned to work of national importance.

Many of the soldiers drafted in the first wave of the draft threatened to desert once the original 12 months of their service was up. The term "OHIO" was used as a protest sign: "Over the Hill in October."

By 1942, a survey found that 69% of high school students favored a draft. (Another way to look at that is almost one in three opposed it.) Between October 1940 and March of 1947, more than 10 million men were drafted. The termination point of service was extended to last six months past the end of the conflict.

Eddy was a sophomore in high school when Japan attacked Pearl Harbor on December 7, 1941.

On December 8, 1941, the United States declared war on Japan.

Three days later, Germany declared war on the United States.

This was the backdrop for the young American men and boys in the early 1940s. There was no escaping the prospect that you could be called upon to go fight in a foreign land. Your friends, neighbors, fathers, and brothers were all affected.

Eddy was no different. In 1941, he turned 15, but his older brother, Bruce, was almost 18 and would be registering for the draft.

17

As a devout Christian, Eddy's position on war was clear. He was against it*. He had been building a path of not just nonviolence, but of outright opposition to the waging of war. He needed to reconcile the struggle between war and peace when the country was dragged into war.

Hinsdale was an upcoming upscale community. It was not a largely immigrant community who looked at the effect that the war was having on the home of their parents or grandparents.

While the church the Edwards family attended wasn't one of the traditional "peace" churches, many churches had, especially at the outbreak of the war, taken a strong non-violence, antiwar approach to the conflict. But the values of a community often evolve outside of the church walls. While there was plenty of anti-war sentiment, there was also considerable movement for the support of World War II.

War was everywhere. From the dinner table to the movie theaters where they showed war news reels, as people went to work, or to the local diner, chances were they were going to run into war news. It filled the pages of the newspapers.

More and more families had members going into the armed forces, either through the draft or by volunteering. At this stage of the conflict, casualties were minimal.

Eddy's views, the ones he articulated in his essay about war, the ones he argued in Miss Cline's social studies class, were increasingly seen as radical. As people formed their positions on the war, it became more than just a friendly debate in the controlled environment of a classroom.

Eddy sensed that his point of view was different than that of many of his classmates.

With some, this led to confrontational encounters. He had friends who, even if their beliefs were somewhat different, stood by one another. Others, however, were looking for a

---

* *The previous year, he had written an essay about his conviction that the draft was unconstitutional.*

18

fight, and who better to pick a fight with than a pacifist? The pacifist dilemma: How forceful can a person be and still stay a pacifist? There were times when logic and words alone were not enough to defend one's position.

The whole world was at war. He found the whole experience unsettling. It made him very ill at ease.

Eddy believed in the power of reasoned discourse. He put together discussion groups at school, giving him and others ample time to express their points of view to all who would listen.

His family situation provided him with an excellent foundation of both information and presentation. At home, he was expected to be articulate and, as the youngest, lost many a debate to both his siblings. Furthermore, both of his parents challenged his academic position. He learned to bring a good argument. He also learned that one of the necessary tools of a good debater was the ability to listen. One needed to listen to one's opponent while at the same time formulating a rebuttal and, in some cases, finding center ground to agree with them.

The discussion group he formed was put together at his lunchtime, which helped keep it from becoming too confrontational. When lunch was over, the discussion was over and it was time to settle down and get to class. Eddy found this a favorable format. No winners, no losers, no one keeping score. He simply hoped to be able to share his point of view and perhaps get one or two friends to rethink their own opinions.

Chapter 5
Circle Pines moves to Stewart Farm

Very quickly, Circle Pines outgrew their residency at Chief Noonday. The lease for the camp almost hadn't happened in 1939 because of government delays, so the Central States Cooperative approved a committee to find a permanent site. They became frustrated by the slow pace of the government's response to something as simple as their rental application. Adding to their frustration was the fact that since Chief Noonday was a new facility, there was no opportunity to build anything.

"We could not even drive a nail into the wall without first getting permission from Congress," said Dave Sonquist.

They knew they needed to find their own space.

An old farm a few miles south of Chief Noonday went up for sale. The committee raised $100 to put down an option but then chickened out of the deal.

The Edwards were one of core groups of families who had bonded to Circle Pines and the co-operative mission. They disagreed with the committee's decision. In what appears to be a unique action in the history of the cooperative movement, they formed a new cooperative camping association to take over the purchase of the new property. By January 6, 1940, the new cooperative pulled together a down payment of $1000 for the farm—mostly from donations from the families.

The old Stewart farm had once been a showcase farm in Barry County. It came with lake frontage, but it had suffered soil depletion and erosion from a century of competitive agriculture, a farming model with no government support or incentives to rotate crops or protect the soil. It was a parcel of 283 acres with a Civil War era farmhouse and other old farm buildings. It was said that the roof of the farmhouse leaked in all 12 rooms, its main floor sagged six inches, its well pumped no water, and there wasn't even an outhouse. Turning the property into a camp was going to be a massive undertaking.

While work on the Stewart farm was underway, Circle Pines continued to lease Chief Noonday for the summers of 1940 and 1941. During that span, the college age volunteers, including Eddy's brother Bruce, re-shingled and repaired the farmhouse, installed a septic system, fixed the well, cleared away the wreckage of what was once the old barn and silo and, on one occasion, assembled a temporary dining hall at the lakeside in five days flat. The programs that ran at the Stewart farm during those years were all work programs, while they continued to run recreational programs at Chief Noonday.

The families of Circle Pines were no strangers to organizing and persuading or reaching out to other groups for help. One of the Circle Pines board members persuaded the Quakers from the American Friends Service Committee to sponsor work camps those two summers. This had a profound effect on the Circle Piners. Every day, they were inspired to drive down the road to "their" camp and find jobs to do. so impressed were they with the spirit and work of the Quaker volunteers. That following summer they organized their own youth work camp.

By 1941, the co-op had attracted the attention of Frank Lloyd Wright. He traveled to the Stewart Farm to inspect the site. He also met with a delegation of Circle Piners at Taliesin, Wright's estate in Wisconsin at the time.

Wright did a number of drawings for Circle Pines, including ones for a new dining hall, pier, bathhouse, amphitheater, craft shop, staff residences, administration building, and numerous cabins[*]. Though in the sunset of his career, Wright appeared to take a keen interest in the working of the co-op.

Everett Sr. was no doubt star-struck, being in a position to

---

[*] *Fallingwater, one of Wright's most famous residences, had been recently completed in 1937, but it is said that he was willing to take a reduced fee to try to help out Circle Pines.*

work, assist, or even collaborate with someone of Wright's stature. Everett's own design work centered on the Arts and Crafts style, likely due to having grown up in the shadow of Gustav Stickley, who started his magazine "The Craftsman" and helped to bring "mission" furniture to the American public. Later, Everett did many drawings for the buildings at Circle Pines and did the design work for the massive stone fireplace which became a centerpiece of camp life.

With Wright on board, there was a hope to quickly expand what Circle Pines would have to offer, with the ultimate goal to have a complete progressive folk school.

For the Edwards family, the start of Circle Pines brought a new purpose to their participation in the cooperative movement. It became not only their summer retreat, where they could send their kids off to camp, but it also provided work and training opportunities for all three of the Edwards children.

As rehabilitation of the Stewart farm progressed, Circle Pines became a destination for work and social gathering weekends throughout the year. It was a place for fellowship. A place to get away from their daily life in the city while working together to rebuild the facility.

There was a stark contrast between life in the city and life on the farm. Even in the '40s, city life was fairly well illuminated. There was a glow from both streetlights and neighborhood homes.

Life at camp or at the farm is where they discovered what natural darkness was. If you were away from one of the main buildings, there was no light, unless you brought one with you. A few years earlier, the Rural Electrification Act of 1936[†] had passed to provide federal loans to expand electric distribution

---

[†] *The funding was passed to cooperative-owned electric companies which bought the electric wholesale and used their own transmission and distribution lines. These were member owned companies, some of which are still in operation today.*

lines to isolated rural areas. However, farms had not yet ramped up a lot of outdoor lighting. Outside work was limited by daylight hours and during fall and early winter, those hours grow shorter by the day.

Chapter 6
Discussion groups and strained relationships at school

I n the fall of 1942, Eddy settled into the routine of life as a student during the school year, with many trips to Circle Pines during the summer and vacation time. Circle Pines exposed him to a larger world of opinions that differed from what he found around Hinsdale.

His high school discussion groups were a good outlet. They provided an opportunity to challenge the beliefs of his classmates, not all of whom disagreed with him. But with the changing climate in the county toward the war, the strain between him and some of his older friends became evident.

Circle Pines had provided him with a new opportunity for friends, some whose opinions were more aligned with his. Even though the families who had founded Circle Pines came from a wider geographic area, from Detroit to Chicago, from Indiana and Ohio and Wisconsin, there were enough from Chicago and the surrounding area for him to find a new group of friends close to home and not feel entirely isolated.

It struck him as oddly difficult how, with a war being fought on two fronts, he had to find a balance between religion and the war. While the world around him was turning right, he was turning left. The direction of the country and its justification was in direct conflict with what he had learned from his religious lessons.

Many in the religious mainstream were also having difficulty reconciling how to present their teaching of love and peace to a congregation whose fathers and sons were serving their country in the armed forces. Many churches, including the one Eddy attended, took an anti-war, anti-killing stance. Some church leaderships began to not only speak out against the war, but also took on the task of assisting those who opposed conscription into the armed forces. While Eddy struggled with the religious connotations of war and killing, his brother Bruce took a more simplistic approach: killing was bad. Therefore, he opposed killing for any reason.

Everett and Viola both stayed active with their various organizations. Though one might argue that some of the organizations were antiwar, they saw themselves more about trying to improve the world they were living in. From the co-op's desire to build a better buying platform, to the American Friends Service Committee, which strived to help those who were being displaced by the war, they were less concerned with the current global conflict, and more worried about the impact wars have on people.

Eddy resisted following the mainstream position of many of his classmates, who were increasingly more pro-war, and pro whatever-the-country-is-doing, as long as they could salute and wave the flag. He was not afraid to voice his opinion and knew he risked being viewed as a radical, especially compared to his conservative classmates. He had become a skilled debater on the issues, but one never won or lost such debates. Everyone just packed up their opinions and moved on.

Beyond the abstract debates about world politics, it was a tense, difficult time to be a young American man. If Eddy looked to his own future, he knew that he, along with his friends and classmates, would likely be drafted. Brothers, uncles, and fathers were already answering the call. The draft had already impacted Bruce, who now faced personal decisions about his future. Eddy knew it would affect him as well, there was no exception.

Though the war was unpopular with many Americans, the boys in school experienced rising nationalism. Eddy watched as his classmates became flag waving loyal "patriots," pounding their chests and beating the drums, though it would be a few years till it was their time to answer the call[*].

---

[*] *It's easy to proudly proclaim how brave you were before it's your time to act.*

25

Eddy looked at things differently. He saw a world of inequality. It's not that he accepted the invasion of Europe by Germany and Hitler or easily turned the other cheek from Japan's attack on Pearl Harbor. He was opposed to all of those actions, but he had a deep understanding that the country was being encouraged to hate a whole group of people because of where they lived, solely because of the sins of their government.

He had "danced the dance of many lands," which provided him with a level of kinship with other cultures. He believed America could benefit from welcoming them all. His moral compass told him what was needed was a way to help these people. Could there not be a better way than to wage war?

Eddy needed to help people, not to hurt them. Even now, at the age of fifteen, he volunteered with his church groups, youth groups, and wherever he thought he could contribute. He could sing, he could dance, and he used the arts to show a positive way of looking at the world.

In school, Eddy did well enough in math, the sciences, English, and physical education,. However, history and social studies classes (again, with Miss Cline) severely taxed his desire to see the world in a positive light. This was the arena he found most difficult, where all his views on government and social affairs were put on display. Those who hadn't been part of his discussion groups found his stance to be outlandish and radical.

He didn't intend to pick a fight, but by 1942-43, the tenor of the country leaned heavily toward the military's position that fighting was the only way to defend what we call freedom. Perhaps Miss Cline singled him out from time to time, knowing that he could provide a counterpoint to how many perceived the general public opinion. Perhaps Miss Cline harbored opinions about the Edwards family from contact with Bruce in previous years. (Bruce's views were not the same as Eddy's but there were enough similarities to group them in the same class.) It didn't matter, Eddy never spoke about Bruce's interaction with Miss Cline. Through the years he had lost respect for her as a teacher and didn't think she liked him much either. Theirs was at best an adversarial relationship and it was in the class that disturbed and distressed him most.

Chapter 7
Trouble and student protest

The start of the '42-'43 school year was a turbulent time for Eddy. Dorothy was deep in her studies off at college. Bruce was making a move to Kalamazoo, Michigan, to attend Kalamazoo College while eyeing his draft status. He had registered for the draft after his eighteenth birthday. However, instead of being assigned 4-E conscientious objector status, he had been assigned a 1-A draft status. According to the law, he needed to appeal for a 4-E classification. The matter was far from settled.

In the summer of 1942, Eddy had written a letter of inquiry and complaint to the U.S. Senate Committee on Appropriations to question why the Broadcasting Corporation had refused to grant Consumer's Co-operative movement on-air time.

On January 9, 1943, he received a response from Senator C. Wayland Brooks.

> Dear Friend Edwards,
>
> Your letter of December 18th relative to the refusal of the broadcast corporation to permit the Consumer's Co-operative movement to purchase time for broadcasting is at hand.
>
> I thank you for giving me your views concerning this matter. I have taken up the subject with the Federal Communication Commission and am awaiting an answer.
>
> With kind regards, C. Wayland Brooks

Eddy harbored a need to become the voice for those whom he

thought stood silent. By the time he reached out to the Hinsdale High administration and Principal Mossman at the school office over the blatantly unfair grading practices of Miss Cline, he was aware that there were growing tensions at the school and was already involved (or at least a tacit participant) in many of the activities the administration found antagonistic. To some, it appeared as if he sought a battle to fight the injustice he saw.

Mossman had taken over the position of principal the year before and was already putting his stamp on how he felt the school should be run. One of his first acts as principal had been to insist on control of all the activities of the student council. Unsurprisingly, this did not sit well with the student population. There was also a degree of frustration among part of the faculty.

At sixteen, Eddy and his classmates took exception to the administration treating them like children. Many students already had driver's licenses. It was an age where an occasional classmate had dropped out to get married, and there were plenty of stories of underage young men who lied about their age to join the service.

While Eddy was far from being out on his own, he had a job delivering newspapers. Every morning before school, from 4:30 to 7:30, he would complete his route. He became aware that many of his ideas and actions had begun to radicalize his thinking and in his words, he noticed a negative personality trait. To have the principal suspend privileges for no other reason than because he could, didn't sit well.

It was a turbulent time, but Eddy happily insisted it all came back to Mossman.

"Mossman was a one-tracked person with very little foresight," he grumbled. "The person responsible for all the bickering at school."

One day Mossman decided to expel a student. Whatever his reason was, the decision caused an uproar with part of the student population, Eddy included. When taken in combination with other grievances, including Eddy's and his classmates' accusations and their grading experiment with Miss Cline, like dominos falling, it set in motion a noteworthy chain of events.

Due to the suspension of this one student, a small group of classmates thought that staging a student walkout as a protest would be an appropriate reaction. Working together the students devised a plan. At a pre-determined time and date, as a sizable group, they would walk out of class, down the hall, and exit the school building, more than likely for the remainder of the school day—a student strike.

As with all plans, the more people you recruit, the more likely that news of your plan will no longer be kept secret. Mossman learned not only the intention, but of the time and place of the walk out. He was determined to both stop the protest and to flex his authority over the school body in the process.

The day for the walk out arrived.

Mid-morning, prior to lunch was the pre-arranged time.

As planned, a large number of students got up from their desks and left their classrooms.

They gathered in the hall, then headed for the main exit doors of the school.

As the doors came into sight, it was evident that Mossman knew of their plan. He was positioned in front of the doors, blocking them. But he had gone a step further: he had brought a chain and padlock with him to school that day. He had securely locked the doors, and only he held the key. He no doubt thought that this would allow him to reign supreme over the protest and show the students who was in charge of the school. Mossman thought he had control of things. He figured the students would have no choice but to return to class and face whatever sanctions he could dish out after the fact.

Upon seeing Mossman and the situation, one of Eddy's friends noted that his family had knowledge of the workings of the local fire department and that the school had recently, for fire safety, not only installed a fire alarm system but had also connected it directly to the fire department so that in case of a fire, the fire fighters could save valuable time in their response. Fire safety was of upmost importance to the Hinsdale fire department after having lost the schoolhouse to fire years earlier.

Someone within the protesting students pulled the alarm. (Eddy always maintained that he was not the alarm puller, but he knew who it was.) This triggered the following series of events—

First, the alarm went off in the school.

This sent the rest of the student body, who hadn't participated in the protest, and may not have even known about the protest, into the halls, looking for an exit.

The faculty hurried to get the students out of the building.

The fire department, having no notice of a planned fire drill, immediately responded to the alarm.

With sirens blaring, the firetrucks, filled with fully dressed firemen, charged to the school, where they encountered a chained set of doors at the main entrance. The firemen took their fire axes and cut through the hinges holding the doors in place, dropping the doors to the walkway in front.

Only then was there an opportunity to try to straighten out the chaos of the last few minutes.

Mossman tried to explain to the fire department why the doors were chained. Meanwhile, teachers focused on getting students and faculty back to their classrooms. Panic, anger, and just plain bewilderment over what was taking place ruled.

In the aftermath, the suspected organizers of the student strike were called up to be interviewed by Mossman. Eddy was one of those questioned, though he always maintained he wasn't involved in making the strike happen. Mossman passed the blame to the student body and continued to exert his control over the school.

In a further show of protest, and with the approval of their faculty advisors, the students disbanded the student council.

By the end of the school year, Mossman had made the decision to fire nine teachers. Band, Art, English, and Drama all lost the heads of their departments. One of the last assignments from Eddy's English teacher was for the students to write an essay on democracy in education. It wasn't long till Eddy found out that Mossman had read his.

Eddy's summer was already planned out. It would be spent working and playing at Circle Pines. The relief from the school year and heading off to camp couldn't come quick enough. But unknown to Eddy, there would be decisions made during the summer which would have a tremendous impact on him.

Chapter 8
Summer of '43 and the move to Michigan

After the upheaval of Eddy's junior year of high school, he was ready for camp. There was a significant amount of work needed at Circle Pines. Even though they had now owned and occupied the grounds for a few years, they were still in the process of repairing what was there and building new.

Eddy didn't mind the work and enjoyed the adventure of all of it, knowing that he would find plenty of time during the days to swim and be at the lake, and evenings would be filled with song and dance.

Meanwhile, Bruce, who was still waiting to hear from his draft board about his status, headed to Lake Geneva, Wisconsin, for a religious youth fellowship conference. After the conference ended, he headed north from Lake Geneva alone on his bicycle—nothing fancy, just a single speed bike packing his sleeping gear and personal supplies.

Bruce visited several destinations, going up through Wisconsin and the upper peninsula of Michigan, and coming back down through lower Michigan. His travel plans included visits to camps for Civilian Public Service, which was a requirement for service for Conscientious Objectors. There were camps in Brule, WI; Lanse, MI; and the Wellston and Walhalla camp in Michigan. By the time he started home, he had logged nearly 1000 miles on his bike.

Bruce felt the best way to determine what awaited him as a Conscientious Objector was to visit the camps to get a feel for what camp life was about and, perhaps to determine a preference if he had a choice of camps. His contact with his family was going to be minimal for much of the summer.

Except for a letter here or there, Eddy did not hear from his big brother.

Eddy's summer had its own twists and turns. Though he didn't know it at the time, the camp director, David Sonquist, was interested in putting into motion a plan for the camp and farm to become operable year around, not just a summer operation.

Sonquist had a vision. Part of this vision was to have a folk school, much like the Danish Folk School. Having invested considerable time researching both the folk school and the makeup of a rural homestead, he thought Circle Pines Center could provide an opportunity to try and make part of his dream a reality. The initial groundwork had been laid when Circle Pines or "CPC" acquired the Stewart farm. It provided a place for a much-needed framework to establish a homestead.

What the Stewart Farm and the camp at Circle Pines provided was both a place and a team of like-minded people who were willing to provide, at least to some extent, a labor force to help form a workable homestead. Volunteerism and a dream of co-operative living marked the very foundation on which to build Sonquist's dream.

As the summer progressed, the camp administrators decided to keep the farm open through the winter. A plan was put forth in which a small number of young people would be allowed to winter at the farm.

Eddy considered the proposal a wonderful opportunity. Both Viola and Everett were agreeable to the thought of a "boarding" school for Eddy. In reality, it was much more than a traditional boarding school situation. Circle Pines was only taking care of the boarding part of the experience. Middleville High School would provide traditional education. But the real education came in the form of all the other parts coming together—group living, rural education, farm chores, and life against the backdrop of the educational background and guidance of Dr.

David Sonquist and his wife, Dorothy.

A total of six students were in the co-ed group. Dwight Knox of Alpena, South Dakota, was the oldest and was put in full time charge of the farm work. In addition to Eddy, the others included Sybil Knox, also from Alpena, Fran Dungan of Downers Grove, Illinois; Lonnie Irvin from Akron, Ohio; and Ralph Dornton from Detroit, Michigan. Everyone lived in the massive Stewart farm farmhouse.

There was a small tuition fee of ten dollars per month, along with the understanding that the students would be actively running and working the farm. Schooling would take place locally

(or as local as possible in rural America). Middleville High School is part of the

Thornapple/Kellogg school system.

Eddy took a preliminary tour of the school. His first impression was very favorable. He loved the ruggedness of the school. He was also impressed by its progressive nature, especially when he compared it to conservative Hinsdale. The ambiance and feel of the set-up meshed with him. Without a second thought, Eddy committed himself to a new life in Michigan.

He needed to take care of a few things before he made the move to Cloverdale, the town name where Circle Pines was located. Besides returning home to pack for more than just his summer vacation, he needed to stop by Hinsdale High School to request a transfer and pick up a transcript of his grades.

Upon entering the office at Hinsdale High, he was told to wait "just a moment." The administrator returned promptly with his transfer, already filled out with the exception of a blank space for the name of the new school he would be attending.

Eddy realized that the Hinsdale administration had no intention of letting him return for his senior year. Papers in hand, he spun around and exited the doors of Hinsdale High one final time.

The coming school year was filled with new challenges and

new everything for Eddy and the others.

None of the students at the farm had their own cars, so the daily 12-mile trips to and from school would be made by bus. Catching a rural school bus meant an early rise time for the long journey which included stops at many homes. It was not uncommon for the ride to last up to an hour for those who were first on the bus in the morning or the last stop in the afternoon.

The students at the farm were old enough to prepare meals and see to their own needs, but there was a much higher degree of fending for themselves, which merely started with getting up and dressed, preparing a good breakfast, and a sack lunch.

At camp, being older campers, they'd already had some experience in the kitchen, but the old farmhouse didn't have a modern cook stove. At the start of the school year, cooking took place on a small coal-fired cook stove in the kitchen. It was smoky and produced excess heat which wasn't necessarily a bad thing during the winter.[*]

A pod of Circle Piners all going to the same school meant they had friends on the bus—a nice thing to have when starting a new year at a new school. Classes were small. Eddy's graduating class had 36 students in it. The following year's class had 29. Very quickly, Eddy found he liked his teachers and his classes. The work on the homestead was hard, but in many ways, his life was easier.

---

[*] *Not until the following spring did they acquire a newer commercial propane stove—of which the camp was in dire need.*

Chapter 9
Bruce and the winter of 43'

While the school year provided Eddy with welcome relief from previous years, there was plenty of drama playing out with the rest of the family.

Bruce had applied for, and been refused, a 4-E draft classification. In the fall of 1943, his hearing was held, all documented by the F.B.I. and reported on.

Bruce was considered to have no particular religious training, though there were plenty of church records for both attendance and participation. Because he didn't lean on his religion as the foremost reason for being an objector, he was seen as not having an "earnest religious interest."

Further complicating things were conflicting reports from interviews with people who were supposed to know him. One person claimed that it was common knowledge that Viola didn't want her boys to go to war and Bruce was just looking to avoid military service. Another claimed there was no parental involvement that caused him to apply for a 4-E classification.

A particularly troubling statement came from Martin B. Travis, superintendent of Hinsdale High School, who had known Bruce for 10 years. He claimed that Bruce did not view himself as a conscientious objector from a religious viewpoint, and if he was applying under religious grounds then he was "yellow."

Travis wrote to the FBI after the report came out, stating:

"I did not have any information whatever as to his religious objections to war...

"I would like to state that such lack of information on my

part could not be interpreted that I had any evidence that he was not a conscientious objector. I note that the report of this interview stated that I called Mr. Edwards Yellow, I do not recall making any such statement. My lack of information regarding his personal beliefs would not permit such a remark."

The hearing officer, while he was impressed with Bruce's honesty and integrity, along with the high standing of an in-person witness, concluded that due to the FBI report, a report which appeared to have many flaws and contained information that was, for reasons unknown, inaccurate, and possibly, fabricated. Bruce was to be denied CO status,

Bruce received his induction notice on November 1, 1943, with an induction date of November 15, 1943.

Bruce refused induction.

It was requested that he turn himself over to the FBI, which he did. He was arrested and released on bail of $1,000.

Meanwhile, Everett Sr. was attempting to get a Reverend Hyslop to meet with the

Department of Justice in Washington.

There was a real consideration of taking Bruce's case to court system. He spent the winter into the spring of 44' finishing classes at Kalamazoo College and waiting for his day in court.

Chapter 10
Stewart farm and the winter of 1943

Back at Circle Pines, the farm was a lot like a new homestead. Up till this time, much of the farm operation had closed down for the winter. Neighboring farmers often helped with field crops, but the farmhouse had only been open for weekend retreats.

As early as 1942, they started with just a small garden, but now expanded the program by acquiring a cow with calf and a pig from Loyal Hoyt, plus two goats from the Dungans. In the fall, the camp purchased a team of draft horses and started acquiring farm tools.

For the farm to be able to prepare crops early enough in the season, in the spring of 1943 they put together a greenhouse. A "we can do it ourselves" mantra and dogged determinism was the rule of the day. Now, with the expansion of the farm program, improvements to the greenhouse were needed. They sourced their own wood for construction from the camp property and were able to get a neighbor to mill the oak into boards. They fashioned oak frames for the greenhouse in their own millwork shop, then attached "cello glass"[*] and made their own stain from pigments in the camp shop. The greenhouse was complete.

The farm program was already in full swing. From the beginning of moving onto the property, there was the desire to have a program that could produce enough food to meet the

---

[*] *The term "Cello glass" was used in a Circle Pines newsletter to describe the panes of glass in the greenhouse. It is possible they used the term for a process of using cellophane applied to glass panes to mimic stained glass. Everett had made a glass divider using this method in the farmhouse.*

needs of the residents, with the ambitious goal of being able to sell the surplus products on the open market.

While the main objective of most small farms is to be able to produce and sell at market, they are generally not faced with providing food for more than the farm family. However, at Circle Pines, the farm family was also the camp family and the extended season camp family.

Simply producing enough food for their own consumption was a huge undertaking.

With the greenhouse, the students were able to raise their own garden plants, tomatoes, peppers, cabbages, and more. One of the members of the Circle Pines Co-op, Mark Anderson, provided instruction and showed how seeds became vibrant plants over the course of the growing season. Mark and others both worked and taught in the garden so the camp population could have the benefit of having farm-fresh vegetables through the entire camp season. Through Mark's effort, all the green vegetables for the summer came from the camp garden.

After the harvest, there was a surplus of produce which was canned or stored. In 1943, they had a supply of about 800 quarts of string beans and tomatoes, along with other fruits and vegetables, pickles, and jams. They were also able to satisfy their debt of a $200 government seed loan for the purchase of that year's seeds through the sale of excess produce.

With fall came a new experience for Eddy and his fellow students. There is something about old farmhouses as the weather gets colder. As the dampness permeates the horsehair plaster walls, there is a slight, not unpleasant[†] smell, especially if the house is cold. It's a unique odor all its own. As the moisture in the air meets the lime-based plaster,[‡] it creates a smell you can almost taste. As the heating season progresses,

---

† *But not particularly nice either.*
‡ *Agricultural lime—not the green fruit limes.*

the smell will slowly dissipate, but it's a smell a person remembers for life.

The Civil War-era farmhouse lacked central propane or gas heating. Heating was done by wood or coal. The property was heavily wooded, so access to wood was not a problem, but firewood needed to be cut by hand and brought to the farmhouse. On one outing, with the help of a neighbor's tractor-powered buzz saw, they managed to cut 5 cords of wood [§] in a single day. Moving the wood was another challenge. There was no tractor, no four wheelers, or other mechanical modes of moving it.

The farm work was done with a team of horses. Neither Eddy nor his fellow students had much experience with horses except through lessons during the summer at camp. They needed to learn how to handle both the care and feeding of the horses and needed to manage running a working team as well. Eddy enjoyed the horses. He never claimed to be an expert, but having had this experience and gaining this working knowledge gave him life-long confidence handling and caring for animals.

When Circle Pines Center took over at the Stewart farm, they had as a centerpiece the enormous old Stewart farmhouse and a few out-buildings. The dream of a camp, farm, and folk school would require a much larger infrastructure. Fortunately, in addition to the new student tenants, Circle Pines patrons comprised a highly motivated and skilled work force with a shared vision of what they could become.

The camp began a program of manufacturing their own line of furniture. Permanent cabins had yet to be built, but the winter months were a good time to stay indoors and concentrate on

---

[§] *While the claim was 5 cords of wood, it was more likely 5 face cords. A cord is a stacked pile of cut wood measuring 4' x 4' x 8', a face cord or "rick" measures 4' x 16" x 8'. 5 face cords is the equivalent of just under 2 cords*

shop work in a more temperature-controlled setting. Even the cold shop was far more friendly during the winter when compared to working outside for extended periods.

The camp owned what they described as "an old farm truck." The truck was not only tasked for farm chores. Circle Pines hosted a Christmas reunion for the young people over the holiday season, from December 28, 1943, through January 2, 1944. The group arrived by train in Kalamazoo and were transported to camp via the camp truck. With a total of approximately 30 young people attending, most rode in the rear of the truck—a cold 30-mile trip.

"Junior (17-year-old Eddy was known as Junior for much of his time at Circle Pines) was in Detroit Thursday to take the truck to get it overhauled by Murry Roth," one Circle Pines newsletter noted. Eddy likely went by himself.** There was no mention of anyone accompanying him on the 150-mile trip.

As the school year wore on, Eddy and the Circle Pines students became integrated with their Middleville classmates. They decided to sponsor a get together with the senior class of Middleville, to be held February 4, 1944, and invitations went out. With a good turnout, Eddy took his classmates on a hike to the lake and then they gathered for a supper of hot dogs, cheeseburgers, and soup. Following cleanup after the meal, they taught square dancing and played games.

Even beyond the senior class, Circle Pines was integrating into the local social network. A community open house followed, and their hospitality attracted many of the locals, curious about their new neighbors.

The farm program progressed. More cows arrived and a robust chicken program was added.

During March of 1944, 300 baby chicks were bought and a new brooder house needed to be constructed. The construction of the chicken house also caught the eye of Frank Lloyd

---

** *Throughout his life, "I'd drive it California" was one of Eddy's favorite sayings. In the case of the old farm truck he probably would have jumped at the chance to fire it up and head West.*

Wright, who was intrigued by the double wall stone construction and provided several suggestions for modifications. At almost every turn in the garden and food program, the expansion required the addition of more specialized space.

Chickens provided not only eggs but a source of meat and added revenue as well, as chickens who were subpar at egg production could be culled. A letter from a co-op in the Hyde Park area of Chicago noted that the chickens were some of the best they had seen. They placed an order for up to 100 a week.

Eddy and his fellow students learned how to account for what the farm produced. They kept track of egg production, graphing output over a several week span. They also charted out the milk production from what had become a small but thriving herd. They showed that for a three month period the herd, now at three head, produced 2079 quarts of milk, providing Circle Pines with 1,117 quarts of milk, plus butter, some cheese, and plenty of cream. In addition, they were able to send an average of gallons of cream to the creamery each week. They were also able to raise enough pigs to keep the camp supplied with pork.

Dave Sonquist wanted to make sure that part of the learning process was more than just animal management and crop production. He reached out to Barry County Agricultural extension agent Harold Foster. As a result, Circle Pines gained a visit from Barry Larkin, of the U.S. Soil Conservation Service. With Larkin's help, and with advice gleaned from several books on soil and agriculture, plans were put into place to best develop the land.

Classmates from Middleville High found it surprising that after a regular day of schoolwork, the students from Circle Pines went home to regular classes on "soils."

The homesteading students put a plan in place to utilize composting and a had desire to remain as organic as possible.

As the goal was to become a working farm year around,

Circle Pines decision makers knew they needed to upgrade from the horse team to a tractor. Through the co-operative movement, they negotiated with the International Cooperative Restaurants of Detroit to loan them enough money interest-free to purchase a new tractor. The payments would be made as much as possible from vegetables grown on the farm.

To buy a new tractor, they needed to go through the County Machinery Rationing Board, standard procedure for war time. However, a friend of the farm pulled Sonquist aside to let him know that they were being given a runaround. They were not on the list of recipients for a new tractor, one of the 58 allotted to their county. Those were being reserved for farms who had over 150 acres in tillage.

The board of Circle Pines understood that they were being discriminated against in favor of the large farming model. Small to medium-size farms struggled to survive as policies favored larger monopoly-sized farm operations.[††]

To help alleviate the problem the lack of a tractor caused, two new horses were sourced from a neighbor. Babe and Birdie were a young pair of mares. Eddy and Lonnie retrieved the horses by riding them bareback back to the camp—a five-mile journey. It took several hours to make the trip, traveling at a walk. Eddy sang most of the way, everything from "The Donkey Serenade" to a variety of cowboy songs. Shortly afterward, a request for donations was put out to the general membership of Circle Pines for any saddles, even old ones which could be reconditioned for use.

For Eddy, the school year of '43-'44 was going by gloriously. There were no battles with teachers. No wars with school administration. He was living as an independent young man. There was hard physical work to be done every day, but in the evenings, there was time for song and dance.

[††] *The Circle Pines Board considered large scale farming "the curse of American agriculture." It would be a while before the farm would see a new tractor. Those involved in agriculture understand that this is a problem which persists to this day.*

He took a particular liking to Fran Dungan, a young woman who was also part of the student group. She was a year younger and part of the class of '45, but a special bond developed between them. When the workday was done, they both had someone to dance with, to sing with, and to talk about their dreams with.

As spring neared, the work shifted. Planting was on the horizon, along with the need to start planning and prepping for another year of summer camp. They began to see more work weekends with other families coming out for a long weekend or just a day. It was a spring of controlled chaos, and Eddy loved being in the middle of it. He was not in charge of anything but himself—but what a change that was from the previous year!

As spring arrived, construction began on a new bathhouse. The Board of Directors agreed upon a design to accommodate 100 people during the camp season. Resources for the project were scarce. The foundation was dug by hand and concrete was poured in small lifts, allowing for the movement of the forms as the building grew in height. The wood was locally sourced and rough sawn. In the piles of lumber, dimensions—especially length—tended to be rather random, requiring digging and sorting to find a suitable board. The entire building was built without the aid of blueprints and with a volunteer labor force. The only instructions were the requirements from the health department of a 4000-gallon septic tank requiring a pit 7 feet wide, 13 feet long, and 8 feet deep—all dug by hand, one shovel full at a time.

As aggressive as the building program looked from the outside, an even bigger building program was looming, with planning being done with Frank Lloyd Wright.

Dave Sonquist had spent three days at Taliesin with Wright going over plans for the expansion of Circle Pines. In addition to agreeing to draw the plans for the camp, Wright had expressed a desire to modify the plans for the central dining hall roof. He proposed a redesign which incorporated flatter gables, much like Taliesin, which in his opinion more correctly matched the contours of the property. He also believed that three sizes of cabin were needed to accommodate the different sizes of groups using the property, stressing a desire for more privacy for the families.

In April of 1944, Sonquist received a telegram from Wright's team at Taliesin that the building plans for the cabins were complete and had been sent to Arizona for Wright's approval, after which the plans would be forwarded to Circle Pines. Payment was not due for the design work until the buildings from the plans were complete.

Towards the end of the school year, the Middleville senior class embarked on their senior class "graduation trip," a chartered excursion open to senior classes across the state. They crossed Lake Michigan on the S.S. South American, also known as the "Queen of the Inland Seas." The South American was a large steam ship, 314 feet long, weighing in at 2662 tons. She sported a crew of 165 and could handle 500 passengers at one time.

Arriving at the Holland port at 5:00 P.M., they traveled through the night to Chicago. Four hundred high school seniors were aboard. The ship provided two dance bands and a series of movies and comedies for entertainment, but Lake Michigan was rather rough. The first night, 22 seniors were seasick.

After breakfast on the ship, the students had a chance to spend all day in the city with a scheduled stage play and dinner to wrap up their time in Chicago. Then they traveled back to Holland overnight and arrived back in port around 6:00 A.M. The return trip was windy and cold.‡‡

On May 31, 1944, Eddy graduated high school. This concluded Dave Sonquist's first year experiment with a rural

---

‡‡ *Some of what is known about the trip comes from a letter Eddy wrote on board to Lee Edwards but never mailed.*

boarding school and keeping the farm open. The farm not only survived, but it also flourished through the winter, growing into an active enterprise.

A few of Eddy's house mates, including Fran, were set to graduate the following year. Sonquist busily made plans with hopes for something much larger. He dreamed of developing into some sort of folk school with a more open and innovative curriculum[§§].

[§§] *Many of those dreams were dashed. Circle Pines was unable to build the facility with the Frank Lloyd Wright plans they had. The dream was just too large. The funding was unobtainable. Perhaps had it happened at a time where the country was not at war, more could have been done. Sonquist continued to dream big dreams, but the reality remained much smaller.*

Chapter 11
Sign up for the draft

O n June 6, 1944, six days after Eddy's high school commencement, the Allies' invasion of Europe began with the D-Day landing on the beaches of Normandie. In 1944, 1,591,942 young American men were drafted. There was no way to tell the effect D-Day would have on the war. Many expected the war to drag on, requiring more and more soldiers to fill the ranks in the armed forces.

Though the school year had been great for him, Eddy looked forward to a summer working as a lifeguard and managing the waterfront at Circle Pines. During the months prior to and immediately following graduation, Eddy put himself through the YMCA certification levels for swimming. His waterfront goal had always been to graduate to the deep end of the pool. As a lifeguard, he needed more. He completed his high-difficulty intermediate tests on June 18, putting him in the YMCA Shark Club, their destination for competitive swimmers.

On June 26, 1944, only weeks after his high school graduation, Eddy turned 18.

On his birthday it was necessary for him to register for the draft. On July 11, 1944, he was given a draft status of Registrar and a classification of 1-A.

Eddy had known this day was coming. He inquired about service if he were to be drafted. He maintained that he was willing to serve in the military if he could do so without carrying a gun and not participate as a combatant. He said he was willing to volunteer for medical training and was willing to serve as a medic.

He was told that he would not be able to be classified as a non-combatant, nor would the Armed Forces train him as a medic. Perhaps if he were to be drafted, they said he could find a way to train as a medic, but he would still be required to carry a firearm and train as a regular combatant.

Bruce's experience had paved the way when he had been informed that the local draft board was only going to hand out 1-A classifications and let the appeal board sort it out.

It was a pivotal point in Eddy's life. Bruce's denial of 4-E classification combined with his arrest as a draft evader left Eddy no questions as to where the path he was on would take him.

Local civilian draft boards were made up of unpaid volunteers who gave out the classifications. It's easy to see how the process could be seen as unfair. Take, for instance, the case of the Heart Mountain Fair Play Committee members who refused the draft. The Fair Play members formed in 1943 and started a resistance movement to sign up for the draft by those who were American by birth but born to Japanese parents who were held in internment camps. Heart Mountain had the highest number of American Japanese citizens who were sent to prison. Not till 1947 were those who went to prison pardoned by President Truman.

Eddy needed to apply for—and would likely need to appeal for—a 4-E classification: conscientious objector (CO).

On July 16, 1944, he filled out Form 47, the application for conscientious objector status.

Form 47 required him to answer questions about his life and beliefs.

In Series 1, he claimed his exemption.

Under Series 2, Religious Training and Beliefs. He encountered the following:

1) Describe the nature of your belief which is the basis for your claim in Series 1. 2) Explain how, when, and from whom or from what source you received the training and acquired the belief which is the basis of your claim in Series 1.

3) Provide all addresses where he had lived, parents' name and address, and parents' place of birth.

Series 4 asked about specific participation in organizations, mostly church related. The government wanted to know which organizations counted Eddy as a member. Where were they located? How long had he been a member? What was the name and address of the pastor or leader of the organization? The form went on to ask for a description of the creed or official statements of said religious sect or organization as it related to the participation in war. He was also asked about his relationship with, and activities in, all organizations with which he had been affiliated other than religious or military.

There were additional questions on a more personal level.

"Name and address of the person on whom you rely most for religious guidance."

"Under what circumstances, if any, do you believe in the use of force?"

He was asked to "describe the actions and behavior in life which in your opinion most conspicuously demonstrate the consistency and depth of your religious convictions."

He was also asked for any time and place that he would have expressed this conviction in public.

The rest of the form dealt with work history and school history, along with asking for a list of personal references.

In response to the form, Eddy included a supplemental sheet to Form 47 Order No. 13148.

He wrote.

Series II

1. I believe in the life of Jesus Christ as an example for which to live. It is said that according to Christ, killing was one of the four highest crimes. He himself won many battles without touching a soul. In all my years of church work and training I have never heard of the use of force.

2. I received my training in the fellowship of youth church conferences, in church activities, in

50

missionary action committee work and in daily life. I have been working in the church youth groups for 5 years prior to this last year. We did a large amount of missionary work at our conferences, and I spent a summer in 1941 in a work camp working with a Friends (Quaker) work camp.

5. There are not one or two specific examples of behavior as religious living should carry into as nearly everything in daily living as possible. I have however,

2 years of Church Missionary Action Committee

2 Sunday School weekend conferences

3 years of Y.M.C.A. summer camp

7 years of perfect youth church attendance (not counting at least 3 years of not perfect attendance)

5 Years of perfect Sunday School attendance

5 years member of church youth clubs.

6. I have several expressions of my views. However, most of them were in small discussion groups. At the time I was in my 10th grade I wrote a theme on the constitutionality of the draft. This, however, is from the legal point of view.

Series IV

2.(c) Until last year I was an active member of the Union Church of Hinsdale. This last year I have been at a farm and have had little, if any, chance to attend a church of that kind. While I attended there, I was under the guidance of the youth pastor, Rev. Ralph Hyslop and the pastor, Dr. Wilfred Rowell. I have had little or no contact with the present pastor, Rev. Vogler.

(d) as was stated above the present pastor of the church is Dr Vogler. However, my pastor was Dr. Rowell and Rev Hyslop. Both addresses are given in references. (e) The Congregational church is a church which relies on the person's conscience for religious guidance. The purpose of the church is not to set a strict pattern to follow, but to direct the student's thinking into the best ways, through the teachings of Jesus Christ and other religious leaders. The churches are set up so that they cannot set a definite pattern as each church is different in its creed. All of them, I believe, do state the fact that "we will exemplify the life of Jesus Christ, love the things he loved, and hate the things he hated."

Eddy's cover letter to Local Board #4, Downer Grove, Ill., dated July 19,1944:

Dear Sirs,

Upon receiving my classification of I-A from my local Selective service board, I hereby place my appeal. I wish to be reconsidered for a IV-E classification on the grounds of religious objection. I will accept Civilian Public Service projects or other work of non-military public importance but must refuse to participate in the armed services or any organization in direct connection thereof.

Yours Sincerely,

Everett L Edwards

Eddy was able to move quickly to secure letters of personal reference from several of the adults who knew the kind of young man he was.

On July 20, 1944, Dr. Hayward, from the International Council of Religious Education wrote:

Dear Sirs,

I understand that Everett L. Edwards Jr., will be coming before your board shortly with a view to his classification under the Selective Service act and that he will ask to be classified as a Religious Objector.

I write to set before you my judgement as to the character and sincerity in holding these views and something as to his church connections and his background out of which his views have in all probability come.

I am sure his pacifistic principles are a natural outgrowth of his home teaching and influences. While having a mind of his own, he has naturally been influenced by his home from early days. With his family he has shared in the social and religious life of his church, in the cooperative movement, in the cooperative camp conducted by the cooperatives, and attending lectures in our own and other communities on public questions including war and peace and with some speakers of the pacifist view. His parents put themselves into the life of the church and the cooperatives with their children and so common views have grown up naturally.

Until about a year ago when he went away to school, he was active in the youth program and other activities in the church. He sang in the choir from boyhood. Before going away, he was the chairman of the missionary committee of the Sunday school. I heard our new director of religious education tell how strongly she leaned upon him in getting started in her new work. The family have always been active in the church, either this at home or somewhere else. I am absolutely certain that his pacifist views are the natural result of life teachings and that they do not have sudden or recent origins. He is, I firmly believe, completely sincere in holding them. While not a pacifist myself, I thoroughly respect him and others who sincerely hold such views and profoundly honor my government in making the right of sincere pacifists to be exempted from military service one of the previous values of democracy for which the war is being fought. If I can be of any further service in considering this case, I will be glad to do so.

Sincerely Yours

Dr. Hayward

A July 21, 1944, letter from Wilfred A Rowell, President of Beloit College, Beloit, Wisconsin:

Gentlemen;

I am informed that Everett Edwards has applied to your board for a classification as a conscientious objector on religious ground.

I have known Everett ever since he was a small boy. His family were active members in the Union Church of Hinsdale of which I was pastor for 23 years. Everett was an interested and active participant in the life and work of the church. He was a regular attendant at the church school. He was a member of the young people's group. He was a member of the choir. At the proper age he became a member of the church. In all of these he was an earnest, active Christian youth. I am convinced that his request as a C.O. on religious grounds is absolutely sincere.

I submit this testimony to you in the hope that you will give it your consideration in your decision regarding Mr. Edwards.

Respectfully yours,

Wilfred A. Rowell

It wasn't only from Church leaders that Eddy was able to get letters of recommendation.

On July 21, Eugene Dungan, of Downers Grove, IL. Wrote:

Gentlemen,

I have been told that Everett L. Edwards of 508 N Grant St. Hinsdale has applied to this board for classification as a religious objector to armed service. As your fellow citizen I wish to commend this request to your consideration.

You have by now met several times this rather rare type of courage which overcomes the reticence of youth and avows a religious belief that forbids a service which most Americans deem necessary, and they reward with honor.

If there have been relatively few religious objectors in our district, there have been more in other parts of the United States. The Congress passed the Selective Service Law to make use of their services as well as that of all others.

This young man is honest and courageous. He is well acquainted with Russell Yohn, of this board's district, who is now, as a volunteer, a victim of Pneumonia for the testing and treatments so that ineffective treatments may be abandoned, and better ones used.

Everett Edwards knows James Cassells, also of this district, who after serving some time in prison, worked in a Civilian Public service camp and is now a volunteer in the same work as Russell Yohn.

These young men have something, something which was recognized by the makers of the Selective Service Law. It is, I believe within the power and duty of this board to consider whether Everett Edwards' belief and his courage are really what the law provides for in the 4E classification.

I need hardly point out to you that a decision which puts a registrant directly into service under the provisions of the law is of greater economical value to our country in war time than a decision reviewed and possibly reversed, or a decision followed by a prison sentence even though service follows after that.

It is, of course, more difficult to know whether a religious belief is sincere than it was under the law of World War 1 to know whether a young man was a member of Friends, Mennonites, or Brethren; but it is fairer to assign to special service all young men whose religious beliefs keep them from going to war than to assign only those who are members of some peace church group. It extends American religious freedom to the person as well as to the group.

Now if there is any question that you wish to ask me

or any way that I can help, please call on me; I'll do what I can.

Respectively,

Eugene Dungan

On July 22, David Sonquist, who had spent the entire past fall, winter, and spring with Eddy, added his letter of recommendation:

Gentlemen,

This is to certify that I have known Everett Edwards for the last seven years. For the past year he has been living here while attending High School at Middleville Mich.

We have had many opportunities of observing Everett in his many activities and of talking to him. As far as I can remember, since Everett has been able to think for himself, he has constantly taken the position of an objector to war. He is a very earnest and sincere young man. Honest in his convictions and very active in young peoples groups. He is an extremely virile well built young man and is willing to embark on any venture, provided that it is accord with his beliefs.

I am fully convinced that Everett is sincere in his stand as a C.O. This stand comes without compulsion. We encourage all young folks to think for themselves. As an organization we have no policy on these matters. We have a great number of our members in the armed forces. This makes us doubly certain that Everett's position has come from his own thinking and has not been forced on him from any organizational influences.

Very truly yours

David E. Sonquist

Director

Circle Pines Center

Cloverdale Mich.

On the same day, July 22, a family friend wrote:

Gentlemen,

Mr. Everett L. Edwards Jr has suggested that I write to you concerning my knowledge of him that bears on him being a religious objector to war. I have known for approximately five years, partly because of our mutual connection with a co-operative educational camp in Michigan; Circle Pines Center, and partly because he is a friend of my children and has visited my home.

During these contacts with him I have occasionally discussed the war problem with him, and I have come to know something of his personality and views. I am sure that he is genuinely sincere in his religious views and that he honestly believes that participation in war to be inconsistent with his views, and therefor wrong. I have known a number of C.O.s and comparison of him with others makes me certain that he is not assuming this position for ulterior purpose.

Looked at from another angle his beliefs require him to take a more difficult path than that of going into military service. It is courage, rather than any form of weakness that leads him to a decision contrary to that of many of his friends and most of his fellow citizens.

E.A. Wildman

R.R.1

Richmond Indiana

Within a few days, on July 24, Eddy received another letter from another church contact.

Dear Sirs,

At the request of Everett L. Edwards Jr. I am happy to write to you concerning his membership in the Union Church of Hinsdale and his activities in the Sunday school and other groups during the time that I served as associate pastor and the Interim minister of the church from 1940-1942.

Mr. Edwards was a regular attendant at the Sunday school having received awards for a number of years for perfect attendance and was one of our most active members in our young people group.

I am certain that his convictions are sincere and assumed on religious grounds, though I have not seen him since the summer of 1942. I am sure that his activities in the church have not ceased. I am glad to vouch for his sincerity and his statis of a bona fide religious objector to military service.

Sincerely yours

Ralph Douglas Hyslop

There were replies from the Selective Service system, perhaps to all who spoke up with letters of recommendation for Eddy. One letter dated August 1,1944, to Dave Sonquist stated.

Dear Mr. Sonquist:

Your letter of July 22, 1944 regarding Everett Luther Edwards, Jr., has been carefully considered by the local board. While it was not considered grounds for reopening the classification, we thank you for your interest in the case.

Very Truly yours,

DuPage County Local Board No.4

Bernie F. Nesbit, Chairman

Perhaps it was just the procedure to acknowledge the letters of recommendation as they came in, but not give them any weight in the decision process for classification. On the same date, Eddy received the following letter from the draft board concerning his next step.

Dear Mr. Edwards,

The government appeal agent will be in this office Friday morning, August 4, 1944, for the purpose of assisting registrants in preparing their statements for the appeal board.

If you wish an appointment at 10:15 A.M. he will be glad to help you with your statement.

However, if you do not wish to keep this appointment and prefer to write your own statement, giving in full your reasons for appealing, please notify us immediately so we may allot your time to someone else. If you write your own statement, mail it to this office not later than August 9, 1944.

Yours truly yours,
DuPage County Local Board No. 4
Margaret H Dern
Clerical Assistant

This notice was mailed to both Eddy's Hinsdale address as well as his Circle Pines address.

The pressure was on. Not only did he need to request the letters of recommendation as quickly as possible, but he also needed to account for the mail going back and forth between the draft board and him. If there was a delay, or he failed to reply in time, his request would be denied.

On August 4, Eddy returned to the city to meet with the agent from the Selective Service.

They assisted him in filling out Form 47 again.

There was some confusion surrounding filling out this form. Part of the confusion stems from the fact that some, if not all, of his respondents for letters of recommendation were already receiving replies before he had his meeting to fill out Form 47. He had filled it out the first time on July 16, but it's possible the draft board viewed this as preemptive and refused to take it into account until his draft status was set. Eddy himself may have considered the earlier version just a sample. In any case, on August 4, he formally filled out the form and attached his additional information so it could become part of his official record.

The letters of recommendation continued to come in. On August 20,1944 P/Fc Steven T Norvell added his letter of support for Eddy.

To whom it may concern- Regarding Everett L. Edwards

Have known E.L. Edwards for the past five years. During that period when he approached maturity and formulated the convictions leading up to his important decision concerning his C.O. to war, I knew his family and his home environment, was well acquainted with many of his friends and frequently had the opportunity to hear his beliefs on war and the use of violence.

It is my opinion that Everett is capable of individual thinking and that his beliefs regarding C.O. to war are his own. Admittedly, any persons belief in such a matter whether he favors war or opposes it, are largely a result of training, most particularly the influence of the home and the church, but surely his thinking has been as independent as it could be for a person of that age.

He is sincere. I know from personal experiences that it is not so very hard to go into the military services, supported by the approval of the entire community, but the cause he has chosen, convicting the censure of society and facing punishment, as if he were a criminal, for the sake of an ideal, is in itself no small evidence of sincerity. He has not chosen to become a C.O. in order to avert Military service. His convictions are an integrated part of his philosophy and have been throughout the years I have known him. He is an idealist, who would like to serve humanity by some means other than by killing his fellow men or entering into any organization designed for that purpose.

He is the type of person that congress provided the 4E classification for.

If I can furnish any further information or be in help in any way, I should be glad to do so.

Respectfully yours,

Steven T. Norvell Jr.

Eddy's summer had been disrupted. He was granted a wide berth to take care of his personal matters while holding his job. His summer employment wound up coming to an end a week early. A decision was made by camp board to close early, due to a fear that there may have been exposure to polio[***] and therefore an added risk to the campers and staff.

[***] *The first polio vaccine was administered in the United States in February of 1954, and licensed in 1955.*

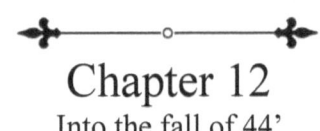

Chapter 12
Into the fall of 44'

Eddy traveled back and forth between Hinsdale and Cloverdale all summer long. He performed his job as the waterfront director at Circle Pines, but with the notice from the Selective Service that his draft classification was 1-A and his need to get ready for an appeal, he had to do everything he could to get paperwork filed by the deadlines provided.

During the summer, Bruce went to trial and was convicted of refusing induction into the armed forces. He was sentenced to three years in the penitentiary and, at the beginning of August had reported to the prison in Sandstone, Minnesota. Eddy was well aware that the road he was following was very similar to his brother's.

With a high school diploma in one hand and a draft notice in the other, Eddy went into the fall of 1944 full of uncertainty. He went back to work delivering newspapers. It was a job: it didn't require much of him, and he wasn't of a mind to try to lay out a career path with everything else going on. Starting college didn't seem like a good idea either. Funds were tight—

Dorothy had just graduated college and Bruce had been in college, though he was now in prison.

The family's resources were drained. Eddy's college plans would need to wait. From fall into winter, his time and energy were consumed with answering to the government and, as quickly as possible, replying to and acting on anything the Selective Service threw at him.

On October 24, the Department of Justice sent a notice of a hearing to be held in Grand Rapids, MI. at 2:00 P.M. on November 6. The notice was sent to Eddy at the Circle Pines address in Cloverdale, MI.

On October 30, Eddy responded to this notice. To be extra careful, he sent the letter registered.

Dear Sir,

I have received notice of my hearing at Grand Rapids on November 6, 1944, and am requesting that it be transferred to Chicago. I find it nearly impossible to come to Grand Rapids myself and extremely hard to have any witness come with me.

I returned to my home address on September 8 to start the job at which I am at the present employed. A notice of the change of address was sent to my local board but has evidently been misplaced. My registration and physical examination were held in Chicago.

Will you be so kind as to consider this request and notify me at the earliest date possible.

Yours very truly.

Everett L Edwards Jr

On an unseasonably warm November 1[*], Eddy received a reply from the Department of Justice, Office of Fred Wetmore, Special Assistant to the Attorney General, Grand Rapids.

Dear Sir,

I have your letter of Oct. 30th requesting that your hearing, set for November 3, 1944 at Grand Rapids, Michigan, be transferred to Chicago.

I have returned the file to the United States Attorney and advised him of your request. Further action will follow, and you will be duly advised of the same.

Very Truly yours,

Fred C. Wetmore

Hearing Officer

---

[*] *Halloween, 1944, was extremely hot and muggy, with temperatures near 80 F*

On November 7, 1944, Eddy's request for a change of venue for his hearing had made it to the desk of the Honorable Roy O. West, Special Assistant to the Attorney General in Chicago.

My dear Mr. West,

There is transmitted herewith the Selective Service Cover Sheet, including the report of the Federal Bureau of Investigation, of the above named registrant, which has been forwarded to this office by Honorable Joseph F. Deeb, United States Attorney for the Western District of Michigan.

It appears that this registrant is presently employed at Hinsdale Illinois, and resides at 508 N Grant Street, Hinsdale Illinois.

It would be appreciated if you would issue Notice of Hearing, conduct the usual hearing and transmit your recommendation to this office at the earliest possible date.

Very sincerely,

James F. McGranery

The Assistant to the Attorney General

On November 13, 1944, Eddy's request was granted, and a new hearing date was set. On Friday, November 24, 1944, at 9:45 am in Chicago, Eddy was to appear in front of the Honorable Roy O. West.

Roy Owen West was a federal hearing officer during World War II for conscientious objector cases. He was 76 at the time of Eddy's hearing and was no newcomer to working in a government position. He had been admitted to the Illinois Bar in 1890, serving as assistant attorney for Cook County, Illinois, and later as city attorney for Chicago. He moved on to serve as Secretary to the GOP National Committee from 1924 to 1928 and was appointed as Secretary of the Interior in 1928 by President Calvin Coolidge.

Prior to Eddy's hearing date, another letter of recommendation came addressed to Hon. Roy O. West.

November 21,1944

Dear Mr. West,

May I add a word of commendation as you meet Everett Edwards for a hearing concerning his 4-E classification for which he is appearing. I have talked thoroughly with Mr. Edwards about his religious background for being a C.O. He came to me because he is a congregationalist and one of our graduates, Rev. Ralph Hyslop, while assistant pastor of his church, was his intimate friend and counselor.

I am convinced that Everett is absolutely sincere in his religious convictions against participation to war and that these are based on deep religious grounds. He has a recorded 7 ½ years of perfect attendance at Sunday school and joined the Union Church of Hinsdale at the age of 15. He has attended several religious conferences, and last winter attended school in Mich. where he worked on a co-operative farm. There he attended Quaker services. I am amazed that his draft board has not awarded him his 4-E classification without appeal, but I hope that you will see that it is done.

Sincerely Albert W. Palmer
Pres.
Chicago Theo. Seminary

Though Eddy had been living away from home for the previous year, now as the youngest child and the only one left at the Hinsdale house, he had to deal with both the uncertainty of his future and the lack of control of his life at home.

There was no way to escape Viola's near constant monitoring of his tasks and her warnings of the consequences of not following through. Though Viola meant well, she could also be totally insensitive to the feelings of others.[†] While she would have concerns for Eddy's mental state, in all likelihood she was blissfully unaware of his anxieties and the pressures he was facing.

Everett Sr. was a much more steadying force. He kept a watchful eye, making sure Eddy's legal progress was on track. The days of living away from parental oversight had passed.

November 24, 1944, was the Friday after Thanksgiving. The weather in the Chicago area had turned cold the previous week. For the week prior to the hearing, daytime temperatures struggled to get above 42 degrees F. Eddy was still busy every day delivering papers, but as the first blasts of winter began bearing down on him, he appeared in front of the Honorable Roy O. West.

The stress of dealing with the unknown was immense. Eddy was acutely aware of how the process had failed his brother. In the cold, Eddy, and his lone witness made their way to the Chicago Loop.

---

† *As a side note, Viola was my grandmother. On the day before my eighteenth birthday, I was summoned to her house. My grandparents lived next door, about 400 feet from my family home. It was the fall of 1972. The war in Vietnam was still going on. I would spend the next year, the year of my 19th birthday, in the draft lottery, eligible to be drafted. I walked over to see Viola for what I expected would be a birthday wish. But no, instead I was handed a group of pamphlets on the current state of Conscious Objector status—what I needed to know from both a religious and a legal sense. So much for a birthday wish from Grannie.*

Taken from the record and transcript of the hearing:
Statement of Facts.

1) Regis. was born June 26, 1926. Education—8 years elementary school—4 years of high school—Employed at Circle Pines Center, Cloverdale Mich. At $17 week as Life Guard

2) Joined the Union Church at Hinsdale on March 24, 1940. He is a patrol leader of Boy Scouts and is a member of other youth groups.

3) Refers to the life of Christ as an example of living. Christ did not use force. Regis. worked in church youth group for 5 years. In summer of 1944 went to a Quaker work camp. Has done 2 years of church missionary action work. He attended 2 sunday school conferences. 3 years of Y.M.C.A. summer camp. 7 years perfect attendance at church. 3 years of near perfect attendance. 5 years perfect S.S. attendance. 5 years membership in church youth groups. Registrant has given public expression to his views. In the tenth grade he wrote a theme on the constitutionality of the draft

4) Believes in the use of force only to restore order. Does not believe in the use of capital punishment. Appeared for hearing. Did not attend church last sunday. Did not attend yesterday's Thanksgiving services. Two weeks ago had a part in a quaker service. Now inclines towards Quaker church. Recalls two fist fights but tried to avoid controversy. Participates in no sports. Has been taught to follow what he believes is right. Does not drink. Does not smoke. Prays and indulges in solitude. Joins in silent grace at table. He impressed the hearing officer as strong alert, frank, and truthful.

5) The regis. introduced a witness who is a con.

minister that while he does not know this regis. except casually, he is an intimate acquaintance with the parents and invironment. Witness declared the Regis. Had 7 years S.S. attendance and is surrounded by a definite Christian influence. He stated that 209 boys of his church are in the service and 2 C.O. After thorough examination of the witness the witness said "I would classify him 4-E"

6) Witness was Dr. Coe of the Oak Park Congregational Church
7) Offered document "A"
8) A summary of the FBI report[‡]

Ref - Knew regis, to be regular in church since 12 years old. Appears to have based his objection on religious grounds. Family always pacifists. Earnestly opposing war. Views have gone beyond that of his church. 2 years ago regis. stated that he did not intend to fight and intended to follow his brother who filed as a C.O. Regis. stand was not taken because of the religious principles of his church. He is of excellent character.

Informant recalled objection by regis. 4 or 5 years ago more personal than because of church

Ref. Sincerity could not be questioned. Is of the minority group in church. Group renounces use of military force. Very faithful member of the church.

[‡] *The summary as provided as part of the official record from the hearing. All abbreviation as done by the FBI was left in context. This was what the Honorable Roy O. West was provided with for information about Eddy's character as seen by his local peers. There were no notes to tell the difference between Ref, Inf, and Conf. Inf (Reference, Informant, and Confidential Informant).*

<u>Inf.</u> Knew Regis. at school. Was not overly religious. engaged in fist fights. Did not mention religion.

<u>Inf.</u> Regis. Had a strong socialistic background. Is lazy. A poor student. More religious than most boys. Is the C.O. type.

<u>Inf.</u> Regis is pugnacious. Went to church and S.S. every Sunday.

<u>Conf. inf.</u> Regis. Is surly and continually in fist fights. Always had a chip on his shoulder. Delights in breaking the rules.

<u>Inf.</u> Is loud mouthed and know it all type.

<u>Former Employer</u> Regis. has no bad habits.

<u>Ref.</u> Convinced the regis. derives his views because of family background. Is steady church goer. And very interested in Missionary Program in S.S. very sincere.

<u>Inf</u> Conversed intimately at Christmas, 1942 and was advised that he was a C.O.
Is sincere and true C.O. type.

<u>Ref</u> Regis. is sincere but had no talk concerning his views.

<u>Ref.</u> Known him 12 years. Very active missionary action committee of church.
Steady church member. Is sincere.

<u>Ref.</u> Religious and sincere. Not discussed C.O.

<u>Ref.</u> Sincere. Is strong in voicing his opinion to selective Service.

Ref. Always had been religious and had taken part in church activities. Very sincere. (Another info. Collaborated)

Inf. Regis does not go to church, but their family does their washing on Sunday.

2 Conf. Inf. Regis. Is not religious—became interested in church when conscription was in congress. Do not believe he is sincere.

Inf. Regis. is probable sincere. Goes to church regularly.

Inf. Yellow

Inf. Is sincere. Has known him for 4 years.

Inf. (2) Never heard him discuss C.O. Are well acquainted.

Inf. He grew up in S.S. Became a church member at 12. He is sincere.

Ref. Known him 7 years. Known generally as a C.O. Very sincere. Objections are based on economic and social reasons as well as religious reasons.

Inf. Regis. sincere.

Inf. Quoted as saying "people with the money are the only ones deriving benefit from war"

Inf. Objections in no way connected to christianity.

Inf. Objection based on religion.

Regis. Has no criminal record

Regis. Has no credit record.

CONCLUSION

Registrant is 18 years of age. Since 12 years has been a member of Hinsdale church. He was reared in a religious pacifistic atmosphere and has a perfect record of sunday school and church attendance for a number of years. He is a member of a church known as the Union Church of Hinsdale. It formerly was congregational. The regis. habits are correct. The F.B.I. has thoroughly investigated the case and has developed conflicting opinions of neighbors, friends, Instructors and others respecting his sincerity. The Regis. brother is in prison as a C.O. The Regis. Has stated that he will follow his example. I questioned the Regis. at length.

Questioned thoroughly a minister of the congregational church who appeared with the Regis at the hearing. I've read carefully a letter attached hereto signed by the President of the Chicago Theological Seminary. I am convinced the Regis. has the religious training and that he is sincere. I so find, since therefor the Regis. has both the sincerity and the religious training and beliefs required in order to sustain a claim for exemption as a C.O., I conclude that he is entitled to classification as such.

*****   ******   *****

RECOMMENDATION

I recommend that the conscious objections of the Regis. be sustained and that he be classified in class 4E and in lieu of induction, he be assigned to work of national importance under civilian direction.

Roy O. West
Hearing officer
Chicago Illinois   Nov. 27, 1944

Chapter 13
The Winter Wait

Dec 4, 1944,

Dear Sir,

After review of the entire file and record of Everett L. Edwards Jr., The Department of Justice recommends in the mentioned case, that your board of appeal, insofar as it concerns the question of C.O. to participation to war, be sustained and the registrant be placed 4-E and assigned to work of National Importance under civilian direction.

As required under Sec.5(g) of selective training and service act of 1940, an inquiry was made in this case, and an appointment to be heard for his claim of C.O. was given to the registrant by the Hon. Roy O. West, hearing officer for the northern district of Ill. His report is enclosed for consideration of your board, this Department concurring in the recommendation he has made.

The attention of your board is called to the fact that the principal place of employment (Hinsdale, Ill.) is in the area of another board of appeal. It is assumed that this case will be transferred to another board of appeal, pursuant to provisions on the amended Sec. 627.13 of the Selective Service Regulations.

If such a transfer is made the foregoing recommendation is intended for the appropriate board of appeal, and this recommendations of the F.B.I. and the report of the hearing officer be inserted into the cover sheet. Under such circumstances it will not be necessary for the board of appeal of transfer refer the file again to the United States Attorney for purpose of investigation and hearing on the question of the registrants claim of C.O.

It would be appreciated if you would advise this office of any disposition made of this case by your board.

The board of appeal which ultimately determines this case of the registrant should advise this office of the classification accorded to him.

Very Sincerely

James P. McGranery

The Assistant to the Attorney General

The letter from James P. McGranery provided a moment of relief to Eddy and his family. The Honorable Roy O. West had found him worthy of a 4-E classification. The F.B.I. had investigated and found him truthful, and when everything was presented to the office of the Attorney General, they found and recommended him to be classified a conscientious objector.

But there was an ominous tone to the letter—something difficult to identify, but enough for Eddy to feel unsure about what the finding of the draft board would be. As noted, there was a question about which board would make the decision, board #4 or board #9. The warning to not disregard the finding of both the FBI and the Hon. Roy O. West meant that such disregard was a possibility and the letter pandered unbecomingly to the draft board about who ultimately made the final decision.

The weather in Hinsdale remained cold. Winter showed its early stages, with daily highs only reaching slightly above freezing and the nights growing colder.

Eddy was still working his job delivering papers and getting up before dawn to start his route. A better job would have to wait until he could get past his dealings with the draft board.

Perhaps he read too much into McGranery's letter, but something in it left Eddy with an uneasy feeling. Having watched his brother go through the process and have the process fail him over the last two years added to his sense of doom. Furthermore, his parents who were deeply entrenched in the anti-war sentiment could not help themselves from persistently advising him on how he should handle his situation.

Eddy's unease began to manifest as a potential illness. He made an appointment with his family's physician, who recommended major lifestyle changes* which included quitting his paper job in favor of better working hours and ideally seeking out a warmer climate.

> Little Cabin in the Woods (traditional camp song)
> *Little cabin in the woods*
> *Little man by the window stood*
> *Saw a rabbit hopping by*
> *Knocking at his door*
> *Help me! Help me! the rabbit said*
> *Or the hunter shoot me dead*
> *Little rabbit come inside*
> *Safely you'll abide*

Circle Pines had long been Eddy's "little cabin in the woods," a place to escape to when life became difficult. When things had gone from bad to worse at Hinsdale High, it had been there for him, a place in the wilderness where he could sing and dance. It was his home as Bruce faced the prospect of prison. It was where he could be a boy but grow into a man. However, Circle Pines was hardly in a "warmer climate," nor did it hold a promise of better working hours.

As the year drew to a close Eddy spent some time conversing with Dave Sonquist, who had taken a keen interest in him and who had acted as a mentor ever since the year he spent at the farm. Winter arrived and with Christmas break

---

* *In the 1940s, there was often a societal expectation that you should just "suck it up" and "be a man about your problems".*

coming up, there may have been a question whether anyone would be at the camp at this time. It became clear that a change was needed— one that started with a new and different job.

Eddy was no stranger to Union Station in downtown Chicago. The Pere Marquette train line was one of the ways he had traveled between Hinsdale, Il. and Cloverdale, Mi. (Though the train wouldn't get him all the way to camp, with arranged pick-ups, it was a good way to travel for a young man who didn't possess his own auto.)

He took a trip to Union Station and made his way to the personal department for the Harvey Company, which handled the food service at the station. Regardless of whether there were help wanted signs posted, he would not have been shy about striking up a conversation. He may have been directed to look for a job with the Harvey House Restaurants located in the station. During the waning years of World War II, there was a shortage of able-bodied men for most types of work. Union Station serviced an average of 300 trains and almost 100,000 passengers each day. The need for help was immense.

Fred Harvey got his start in food service by beginning a partnership with the Atchison, Topeka, and Santa Fe Railway in 1878. By 1889, he expanded his services when the railway gave him exclusive rights to manage and operate his eating houses, lunch stands, and hotel facilities upon the Santa Fe's railroads west of the Missouri River, later expanding east to Chicago and Union Station. The Harvey House Restaurants took pride in their first-class food, service, and cleanliness.

In 1944, Union Station boasted two Harvey House Restaurants, both on the main floor near the concours. The main room was 85' wide by 111' long. There was a lunch counter with three long counters creating an E shape, all done in a combination of green Vermont marble for the counter tops and Tennessee marble for the floors. Walnut wainscotting gave the walls an elegant look. There was also a smaller dining room where travelers had a choice of higher end dinner entrees not found at the lunch counter. While there was space for the main kitchen to service the dining room on the street side of the restaurant, Harvey Company had an area directly beneath the restaurants in the basement that provided refrigeration, freezer, and storage space. There was also office space to both manage the day-to-day running of the restaurant and to house a personnel department.

Eddy secured a job with the Harvey Company. It's likely he could have had a good job at Union Station. That would have satisfied the recommendation of his doctor to find better employment, but it wouldn't have addressed the suggestion of a warmer climate.

The Harvey Company was a huge company with restaurants stretching from Chicago to the West coast. It was a key player in creating a network of eateries for the traveling public, dotting the main routes with both places to eat and places to stay. The company not only had its key city restaurants, but it also had the franchise for food service on the premiere train running back and forth from L.A. to Chicago and Chicago to L.A.: The Super Chief.

The Super Chief was the flagship of the Atchison, Topeka, and Santa Fe Railway. It was named "The Train of the Stars." With a distinctive Santa Fe paint job of red with yellow and silver accents, known as the "war bonnet,"[†] it could complete the 2,227-mile journey between the two cities in 36 hours and 49 minutes, averaging 60 miles per hour and sometimes hitting 100 MPH, though during the war years the speed was reduced and the trip time was extended to just under 40 hours. By 1938, it was running twice weekly and by 1948, daily. It had gained a reputation for Hollywood clienteles and gourmet meals in its Fred Harvey diner cars.[‡]

[†] *In 1937, Santa Fe purchased new "Streamliner Series" diesel-electric locomotives and the red, yellow, and silver "war bonnet" paint was adopted for the new trains.*
[‡] *One year earlier, on Dec 15, 1943 Jazz Pianist Fats Waller died of pneumonia aboard the Super Chief at the age of 39.*

The train was equipped to handle 150-200 passengers per trip. The basic layout of the train was as follows:

EMC E1A Locomotive,

EMC E1B Locomotive #3A,

Baggage-Dormitory-Buffet -Lounge,

Sleeper (17 roomettes),

Sleeper (8 sections, 2 compartments, 2 double bedrooms),

Sleeper (4 compartments, 2 drawing rooms, 4 double bedrooms),

Fred Harvey Diner (36 seats though some were convertible to 48) Dormitory-lounge

Sleeper (4 compartments, 2 Drawing rooms, 4 double bedrooms),

Sleeper (8 sections, 2 compartments, 2 double bedrooms),

Sleeper-Lounge-Observation (4 Drawing rooms, 1 double bedrooms)

Pullman handled management of the sleeping cars, but the cars were owned by Santa Fe. The cars all received names chosen to commemorate Native American tribes, pueblos, and cities along the rail lines.

Standard operating procedure coupled dining cars to a lounge car. The bar/lounge area provided a waiting area for the dining car. It also provided a dormitory area for the crew of 3-4 cooks (chefs), 6-7 waiters and other staff.

There were a number of meals that needed to be prepared and many passengers required table service for the two-night/one-day trip. Eighteen-year-old Eddy, who was never lacking in confidence, and more than likely used his time cooking at the camp plus the year he spent working and living at Circle Pines as his resumé, got a job as the third chef on the Super Chief. He no doubt received a crash course in cheffing prior to the train departing Union Station, but what is most curious is—until desegregation, the staff aboard the Super

Chief was thought to be all Black.§

For the rest of his life, Eddy was extremely confident in the kitchen. He would take charge of getting the first meal of the day ready for the family. An early riser (a remnant of his paper route), getting up, getting the coffee started, and getting grills running was something he always understood. He was a man who knew how to run a kitchen, who knew how to cook. As the third chef, Eddy was probably only left in charge of the kitchen during the less critical times. The kitchen and dining car were open throughout the entire trip, so someone down the seniority list had to be on duty through the night and into the dawn.

The dinner service on the Super Chief was extensive.

Entrees from a typical 1943 menu:

Fish and Entrees (To order)
    Grilled Columbia River Salmon Steak
    Maître d'Hotel, Pomme Rissole
    Broiled whole live Baby Lobster
    Melted Butter, Mexican Slaw
    Lake Superior Whitefish
    Hoteliere, Combination Salad
    Broiled Fresh Shad Roe
    Hashed Browned Potatoes, Cucumber Salad
    Selection of Fresh Vegetables
    Poached Egg Hollandaise
    Union Station Salad Bowl with Julianne of Turkey, Sliced Egg
    Brie-Denzer Cheese, Nut Bread Finger-Sandwich
    French Pancake, Suzette, Currant Jelly

_____

§ *To be a Pullman Porter or wait staff aboard the train was considered prestigious employment. In later years, Eddy often spoke about working with an African American staff while aboard the train. Though he came from a white community, he had been exposed to other cultures at Circle Pines—a true forerunner of an integrated America.*

Grilled Fresh Mushrooms on Toast, Pomme Rissole

Table D'Hote Dinner
Whole boiled live Baby Lobster, Drawn Butter
Colorado Mountain Trout Sauté, Meuniere
Grilled Shad Roe, Maitre d'Hotel
Grilled Tenderloin Steak Sandwich on Toast
New Asparagus, Poached egg on Toast with Julienne of Chicken a la Reine
Omelette Filled with Chicken Livers and Mushrooms au Maderia
Selection of Fresh vegetables with Poached Egg, Hollandaise

This, plus a selection of appetizers, soups, and salads, desserts, fresh vegetables, cheese, and an assortment of relishes. While menus would vary from month to month and year to year, the Super Chief prided itself on serving first class meals. The Fred Harvey Company wanted to not just have good food, but the best you get while riding the rails.

The work was not easy, and mistakes were made. When he asked how to dispose of the food waste, Eddy was told, "just throw it out the door."

Eddy took the instructions seriously and did just that, which in turn covered the side of the train with slop.

He worked in 20-hour shifts. In just under 40 hours, he would complete one train run, in a cramped work environment unlike anything he had encountered before. There was no rest and no way to escape. He was totally exhausted.

Upon arrival in L.A., it's unclear whether he quit, was fired, or just disappeared into the background but his adventure as third chef on the Super Chief was short-lived.

"Dead tired and very sick" were his words as he described the experience later in life. However, instead of being alone and stranded in Los Angeles, he had friends there—probably thanks in part to Dave Sonquist who had several years of building contacts all over the U.S. Perhaps the job on the Super

Chief was nothing more than a way of transportation to the West coast, and the warmer weather the doctor ordered.

While Eddy was out west, Bruce, still at Sandstone, was reclassified as 4-E. With the new classification, he was able to request parole. He asked to transfer to the Civilian Public Service Corps and was placed into a position at a hospital in Ann Arbor, Mi.

There was widespread criticism of the procedure the Selective Service used in which they sentenced a draft evader to three years in prison, only to change the classification while in prison and grant parole and induction into Civilian Public Service.

With the turmoil over Bruce's changing situation, Eddy's family may not have been aware of where he had gone.** It's also possible that they knew and they arranged the place for him to stay in L.A.

In any case, after a few days of recovering with friends, Eddy began to feel his health change for the better. He decided to hit the road and not overstay his welcome.

With six dollars in his pocket, and no apparent plan, he stuck out his thumb and made his departure from L.A. It was mid-December. Though it was snowing at home, the temperature in Los Angeles was in the mid-60s. He had found his warmer weather, however briefly.

First stop: Mexico.

** *Perhaps that was the point.*

80

Chapter 14
The Way Home

For generations many a story has been told about Tijuana, filled with bars and brothels. It's a suggested destination for young men looking for adventure. Eddy was a teetotaler. Having only 6 dollars in his pocket would not have gotten him very far at any establishment.

Perhaps on some level, this was a scouting trip. Or maybe it was to just prove to himself that it was a move he could take. In later years, he never discussed it other than to say, "Yep, went to Mexico."

He didn't last long. Soon he used his thumb to take him home.

With winter settling in across the nation, hitching across a southern route seems most likely. Major roads hold a better chance for obtaining a ride. It stands to reason that the route he took included much of what we call Route 66. John Steinbeck dubbed it the "Mother Road" in 1939. US 66 was the primary route heading East. Running from San Bernardino, CA. to Kingman, AZ., Eddy could have followed it all the way to Chicago.

Route 66 was packed with small towns, diners, and both rural and city life. It contained a much higher traffic count than side roads had to offer. More traffic meant more opportunities for him to hitch a ride.

Crossing the lower mid-section of America through Arizona, New Mexico, Texas, Oklahoma, Kansas, Missouri, and into Illinois was a 3000-mile journey. It took him seven days to cross the country, seeing several cities and towns, and meeting what he termed "many interesting people."

Christmas season began while Eddy was on the road. He

arrived back home on Christmas Eve.

Returning home with stories of his travels, Eddy felt like a new man. He said he was "feeling very good" and noted that all his nervousness had gone away.

The day after Christmas, 1944, the letter from the draft board—Appeal Board No.9 in Aurora, Il—arrived. Raymond E. Shea, Member, informed Eddy that on December 14, 1944, the Appeal Board had voted four to one to give him the Classification of 1-A, denying a 4-E classification and refusing him the right to serve as a conscientious objector.

Eddy stayed home no longer than the holiday. He was off to Circle Pines, his "little cabin in the woods" at least to celebrate the New Year. There, he would have the opportunity to go over his adventure with Dave Sonquist and to thank him for any help he'd provided. Plus, Fran Dungan was one of the students who was still living at Circle Pines. All of them spending the holiday together was the best way Eddy could think of to bring in the new year.

While in Michigan, Eddy sent the following telegram to the Selective Service Appeal Board:

Dec. 29,1944 Selective Service Board 4

1004 Burlington Ave.

Downers Grove Ill.

Notice of classification received from appeal board. I request an appeal to the President. Please take no further action. Will be in Downers Grove by

Tuesday Jan 2, 1945

Everett Luther Edwards Jr. 131

By this time, Eddy had become savvy to the different avenues of recourse he had at his disposal. During the summer and fall, he'd gathered information on what procedures he may need to lean on in the case his classification wasn't granted. He had become quick at making decisions and taking a course of action. Just four days after New Year's Eve, he sent a letter to General Hershey.

General Lewis Blain Hershey was named as the second director of the Selective Service in 1942. An Indiana boy, raised and educated in the state, he had been a career military man since 1916, when he was sent to the Mexican border as an enlistee in the Indiana National Guard. In October of 1940, he was promoted to brigadier general by President Franklin Roosevelt and was subsequently named executive officer of the Selective Service. As director, he tried to keep a fair and compassionate hand in dealing with conscientious objectors during World War II, something he felt hadn't been handled well during World War I.

Eddy wrote.

Sir;

On Dec 26 1944 I received my notice of classification from the appeal board, of 1-A by a vote of four to one. I find I cannot accept this classification as contributing to the war effort is inconsistent with my beliefs.

Enclosed in my file you will find a report from the hearing officer, the Honorable Roy O. West and his recommendation that I receive my 4-E classification.

I have examined my file and find no evidence which would warrant a refusal of my 4-E classification.

In view of these facts would you kindly review my case and appeal to the president on my behalf.

Sincerely

Everett Edwards Jr 13148

With battle lines drawn, Eddy moved beyond just a letter to General Hershey.

He had found an organization in Washington D.C. that was set up to help cases like his: The National Service Board for Religious Objectors. Originally founded in 1940 by three of the peace churches as the National Council for Religious Conscientious Objectors, it became the NSBRO after merging with a similar organization, the Civilian Service Board later the same year. During their first year, an additional 15 groups joined the NSBRO. In 1944, that number had grown to 39.

The NSBRO acted as a sort of clearing house for the COs. They first helped while a CO was trying to get a classification of 4-E. But the organization reached far beyond that.

The NSBRO was divided into three sections.

The Camp Section worked on selecting sites for Civilian Conservation Corps facilities, where a CO would be assigned and would live while performing their work of National Importance.

There was an Assignment Section, whose job was to match the COs with camps and units. They kept detailed records of the men who were assigned and served in the Civilian Conservation Corps, along with the project they worked on, when it was completed, and what work they were assigned.

The last section was the Complaint Section. Their first function was to work with the men who were denied 4-E classification and conscientious objector status. This section would be Eddy's first stop.

Later, an Advisory Section was added to follow changes in the Selective Service laws and regulations. This acted as advisory board to help interpret how any changes may affect the men, even for those who chose prison over going to a CPS camp.

On Jan 5, 1945,

Dear Sirs,

On Dec 26, 1944 I received my 1-A classification from the appeal board even though the hearing officer the Honorable Roy O. West had recommended that I receive a 4-E. My file is now going to Washington on a Presidential appeal. I am forwarding to you a copy of all my letters of recommendation, plus a copy of the hearing officers' report.

Also enclosed is an outline of dates and activities since June 26 the date of registration. Would you be so kind as to see that the letter addressed to General Hershey gets to him, or the proper office. You may keep

the files I have a duplicate here at home. It would be much appreciated if you would see that my case is reviewed and inform me of the next procedure.
Sincerely yours
Everett Edwards

Eddy knew that his outcome was in the hands of others. Depending on what decision they rendered, he was at his last legal juncture. Because of Bruce's experience he knew prison was an option and after his recent trip to Mexico, he knew that skipping the country was also an option.   While awaiting the decision on his fate, he took a trip to the Chicago loop and met up with some old friends. He had many stories to share from his adventure-filled fall.

One of his friends worked at The National Co-operative. Eddy was able to get a personal recommendation. The Co-operative was hiring, and he landed a job as an office boy on the spot. Compared to his job delivering papers, Eddy embraced this new employment and felt the job suited him wonderfully. It was a job he hoped to stay in for a while.

Chapter 15
Draft decision 45'

It was winter in Chicago, with the Windy City's typical wayward weather. January 1945 was brutally cold, hitting -8 F overnight, only to have it bounce back to 40 four days later.

Eddy, now in his new job, needed to make a daily trip into the city. Public transportation in the Chicago area was in a transitional period, but there were many options available to a young man who owned no car. Companies were scrambling to find ways to turn a profit. There was a trolly system, which was beginning to be replaced by the newly formed Chicago Transit Authority (CTA). The El, the elevated train, was already a mainstay of travel around the city and there was always a possibility of hitching a ride with Everett Sr., a friend or co-worker. But even with the cold and additional travel concerns, it sure beat getting up at three A.M. to go deliver papers.

Eddy was extremely personable and was happy to engage anyone in conversation. He loved to tell a good story or share a thought and was more than happy to listen. People sought him out. With his boyish charm, his abundant dark hair, and sterling blue eyes, many found him captivating. At eighteen, he was still youthfully lean but muscled from his year of living on the farm and the combination of his love for both folk dancing and swimming. At five foot eight, he didn't tower over or intimidate co-workers. His wealth of experience gave him ample areas which he could converse on with relatively sound points of view. The job of office boy was a relatively good fit for him, especially since it might have opportunities for him to advance. During the winter of '45, the effects of the D-day invasion had echoed in a new optimism across America.

Perhaps this change in public perception aided Eddy in his personal outlook, though he knew that if the war were to end, it still would not change his draft status or his position on conscription.

February, which can be filled with storms and lingering cold, was unusually mild in 1945. By the time March rolled around, daytime highs were in the upper forties to low fifties.

March 14 was the first 70-degree day of the year. It was also the date on the first document in Eddy's file concerning his appeal.

March 14, 1945

Dear Everett,

I am happy indeed to know that you have actually received a IV-E classification from Washington. You should have had it locally, and I am very happy to have the stand I took reinforced by the Washington headquarters.

You will find many problems in Civilian Public Service Camps, but I hope that you will recognize that they represent a very important creative opportunity for pacifists to demonstrate that they want to serve, if they can only do so in non-military fashion. Just so far as the C.P.S. Camps can make a good impression on the country, they will help secure more considerate treatment for Conscientious Objectors in all future legislation. Cordially yours,

Albert W Palmer

Chicago Theological Seminary

A week later, he received a letter from the Congregational Christian Committee on Conscientious Objectors.

March 23,1945

Dear Everett,

Word has come to me from the National Service Board in Washington that you will be leaving soon for a C.P.S.

camp. As Chaplin of our Congregational C.O.s, I am making an effort to become acquainted with every person who is assigned to C.P.S. I feel somewhat acquainted with you now through your sister Dorothy and trust that you will pay us a visit here at the office before leaving. It may be that I will be able to drive through Hinsdale before you leave but traveling much of the time leaves far too little opportunity for us to make personal visits in the Chicago area.

You are more fully aware than many fellows who are inducted into C.P.S. of both the inspiration and the difficulties of such a life. Realizing that this is both a difficult and unpopular assignment, I feel all the more eager to be help any way possible.   I trust you will let me know as soon as you arrive in camp so I shall have your new address and will be able to write you there. Your suggestions and criticisms of C.P.S. and most of all of our Congregational C.O. Committee endeavors will be most welcome.

I bid you God's speed and trust you will take every advantage to increase your fellowship with both men and God.

Sincerely yours,
James C. Mead
Chaplin-Secretary

Eddy's file contains no other notifications. Perhaps he received a phone call, or the local draft board was issuing a snub, or perhaps he misplaced the paperwork. It might be that though his 4-E classification was granted in March, official word and processing didn't come down the channels until April.

In any case, on April 10, 1945, he received his order to report for his preinduction physical examination, only 6 days later. The order contained warnings that if he failed to report, he could be inducted immediately into the Armed Forces or jailed. After the physical, he had the option to be immediately inducted or to be returned to his local board.

On April 16, it was determined that he was declared physically fit and acceptable for military service, or in Eddy's case, work of National importance.

On May 16, 1945, Eddy received a Western Union telegram from the NSBRO.

> Please wire 941 Massachusetts Avenue N W collect immediately whether you prefer a camp administered by friends, brethren, Mennonites or government no reply will result in your assignment to government camp
> National Board for Religious Objectors 1:35 PM

Two weeks later, on June 2, 1945, came the notice to report.
Dear Sir,

> We enclose herewith your order to report for work of national importance. You will leave Downers Grove at 8:57 P.M. via C.B & Quincy R.R. and will arrive in Wellston, Michigan at 11:08 A.M. on June 20. You will call the local board office on June 19th at 10:30 A.M. for your transportation and meal requests and instructions.
> Yours very truly
> For the local board
> Florence H Kelly   Clerk

Eddy now knew his fate—it would start with a fourteen-hour train ride.

He also obtained the special routing instructions, dated May 25, sent from the Selective Service system in Springfield, Ill., sent to the DuPage County local board #4 in Downers Grove. The instructions stipulated that he would start out on the Chicago, Burlington & Quincy RR and transfer to the Pere Marquette railway to travel to Michigan. Total one-way coach fare was $6.69. He would be granted a request for breakfast in Grand Rapids, not to exceed $1.

On June 2, Eddy received a welcome letter from Earl S. Garver, director of Camp Wellston.

Dear Everett,

We have been informed by the National Service Board for Religious Objectors that you have been assigned to Camp Wellston, and that you will arrive here June 20, 1945. If you will let us know whether you are coming by bus or train, and the hour at which you expect to arrive, we will plan to meet you at the station.

Accompanying this letter you will find some mimeographed materials which describe the camp and the camp program, and which will give you some indication of items to bring with you. If you have any questions after reading this material, please feel free to write for further information.

We are sorry that you are being drafted and thereby forced to leave your home community and normal family life. In fact, we are sorry anyone has been subjected to the draft law, but since our feelings on this matter have not seemed to influence the activity of Selective Service, we have decided that the commonsense procedure is to make the most of opportunities which we have. I dare say that this is a conclusion you have already reached, so I will merely assure you that we at Camp Wellston will do our best to aid you in making your stay here on of service to your fellowman and of profit to yourself. Although we sincerely regret that you are to be drafted, we are glad that you have made the decision to become a CPS man, and we want to use this opportunity to give you an advance welcome to Camp Wellston.

With best wishes, I am

 Sincerely yours,

Earl S. Garver

Camp Director

The appeals, decisions, and waiting were over. Once again, Eddy was off to camp. He had spent most of his life going off to camp, but this was different.

Wellston was known officially as CPS Camp No. 42. Located in Wellston Michigan, it was located 20 miles east of Manistee in the heart of the Manistee National Forest, 116 miles north of Grand Rapids and 304 miles from Hinsdale. Wellston was a small rural community with a population of under 300. Camp 42 was a forest service base camp. It was opened in 1942 when CPS camp No. 17, also known as Camp Manistee, in Stronach Michigan closed.

It was not unusual for CPS camp to close and to move the men around to different locations. In 1943, CPS camp service number 30, Camp Walhalla in Walhalla, MI., closed and several of the men relocated to Wellston.

The camp was run by the Brethren Service Committee. Their main purpose was to have a crew of men to fight fires and engage in fire protection, along with maintaining the firefighting equipment.

Many CO's were scattered around the United States as forest-fire fighters. Smoke jumper crews in the western states lost a substantial number of young men to the draft and the CO's stepped up to fill those positions till the end of the war.

The men at Wellston were a mix of religious affiliations. Nearly 40 percent had enrolled in or graduated from college. Men were both married and single. In addition to fighting fires, they were credited for planting over 1,566,000 White and Red Pine trees, covering more than 1400 acres over a two-year period from 1942 to 1944.

In a way, they became the guardians of our national forests. There was a significant effort for reforestation. They trained in the control of tree diseases. They became involved in surveying the forests and trained as "timber cruisers" to help plan for future cutting.

The job of timber cruiser involved identifying, counting, and measuring stands of timber. It was of keen importance because the war effort required a sizable amount of timber to be harvested in a very short amount of time. Wood of all types went into all parts of the military machine. Gun stocks, pallets, tent poles, paper, boxes, even the PT boats were made from wood. It was the timber cruisers' job to identify what kind of wood was available. In case of emergency, the government knew where to harvest quickly.

There was more to life at camp than only field jobs. For the men's down time, there were a variety of discussion groups covering all manner of subjects. Continuing education classes, much like those offered at a junior college were available. There were job training sessions, with an emphasis on cooperative living and working. The Brethren were joined by the Cooperative league to sponsor a School of Cooperative living, though some men voiced concerns and complaints that it was nothing more than "socialist" thought. In the true spirit of learning to understand your neighbor, there was an interdenominational program known as "My Credo" where men could present experiences based on their own faith, and work on service projects with area churches.

This was no summer camp, however. All was not well at Wellston. The men were still separated from their families, with no benefits or protections of the GI bill that were afforded to those who served in the armed forces. Even though they were drafted into service and the service was listed as "of great national importance" they would have no standing. Some men expressed problems with the work, especially agricultural work. Married men had a hard time supporting their families and asked for changes. Some asked to be placed where there was accommodation for wives and children. Others wanted to be allowed to work their own family farms under the direction of CPS.

But there was also a bigger issue of wages, including questions of what wages, if any, were paid to the CO's, and how those wages were kept or distributed. There were times when a objector could work to earn a wage, but the "work of national importance" was unpaid. Some members of Congress believed that anyone drafted into the CPS was a conscientious objector and therefore was the same as a criminal.

In April of '45 only a few months before Eddy arrived, the men at Wellston staged a hunger strike to protest the conditions. This was vastly different from the camp life Eddy was used to.

Chapter 16
Wellston Part 1

On June 19, 1945, the day of Eddy's departure, the weather in the Chicago area was a summery warm 79 degrees. Most of the trip was aboard the Pere Marquette Railroad* which ran daily from Chicago to Grand Rapids, MI. Even though it was a 176-mile journey to the other side of Lake Michigan, Eddy discovered that the weather was the same.

He spent his allotted dollar for breakfast in the station in Grand Rapids as he awaited a ride to take him to Wellston—a 116-mile trek through the heart of Michigan, through massive pine forests. The scenery was a stunning offset to the anxiety he felt.

CPS camp 42 was like most government facilities at the time. The U.S. Forest Service had the advantage of having good architectural services design camp buildings in a manner keeping with both local materials and the local labor force. At least in Michigan, there was a sameness to the building. In some respects, Eddy found this reassuring. His first exposure to this style of architecture had been at Camp Noonday, a federal facility created in much the same manner with solid utilitarian construction. This was not some high-end resort, but it was a permanent encampment—way beyond living in a tent city.

The camps had to be able to move men into and out of the both the facilities and the work they performed. Because COs were the exception and not the norm, the men came in small batches. Wellston was in operation for less than 5 years. In that time, 633 different men passed through their doors and worked

---

* *Pere Marquette was the early name for Ludington, Mi. and was named after a French missionary and explorer, Father Jacques Marquette, who arrived in the area in the mid-1600s, died in 1675, and was buried there.*

from the camp. Whether because of assignment, the specialized needs of a particular area, or not fitting in, the men moved about.

Eddy had no way of knowing that his future brother-in-law, Barney Aldrich, who was also a CO, also passed through Wellston, along with stints in the western states, and was now stationed in Chicago, trekking through three and half years of service to his country.

No universal term applied to the COs who were drafted into work of national importance. Had it been the Army or Navy, "soldier" or "sailor" would have applied, but they were looked upon as just workers. For many, their position was looked down upon. They were the cowards, the unfit, the un-American boys who wouldn't go fight. It was a stigma COs knew, yet their deep convictions, no matter how unpopular, made them willing to be assigned to camps as workers.

To help him deal with both anxiety and his new status. Eddy kept a diary during his first five weeks at Wellston.

Weds. June 20
Arrived at C.P.S. Camp Wellston at 12:00 noon. Roscoe Swank (from Ohio) & I arrived at the same time. Met at train by Paul Nelson. Afternoon spent in loafing and sleeping.

June 21
Took a tour of the camp today with the other new fellows.

June 22
We cleaned up cabin. So top grohes [†] 6 new fellows. Afternoon we had some classes. In the evening went swimming & had shots.

[†] *"Grohes"? No idea, because this was copied from a handwritten journal, sometimes there is no telling what exactly the words were supposed to be.*

June 23
On S.Q.[‡] read all day

Sunday June 24
Read today—No work

June 25
Cleaned cabin through. Afternoon classes—arm sore from shots

June 26
Went to Manistee for medical exam. You vaccinated for small pox. Worked on lawn in the afternoon.

June 27
In the morning we cleaned the recreation building and had a game of pool in doing so. This afternoon I did some mimeo work for the camp newspapers.

June 28
Letter today from Mom & card from dad @ C.P.C. Had movie The Glass Key tonight. Roscoe & I swam after supper & I had to pull him out. Worked on project of pulling cones in tree plantings.[§]

June 29
This morning had a bull session on "why C.P.S," It was a good session and we arrived at many decisions. It will be

---

[‡] *Possible shorthand for "stay quiet"*
[§] *The Glass Key was a 1942 movie written by Dashiell Hammett starring Alan Ladd and Veronica Lake about a corrupt politician and a murder.*

Roscoe, perhaps, was not ready for the deep end of anything and was lucky Eddy had spent so much time as a lifeguard.

As for pulling cones, much of the work that came out of Camp 42 revolved around trees. Pulling cones was a form of pruning of the pine trees, removing excess pinecones.

strange to see the difference between our ideas now and later after we've been here awhile. I did some mimeo work today and read another book. Tonight we are scheduled to have our second shots for Typhoid fever. Met Mr. & Mrs. Garver today. Very nice people for directors. Alfred Ames from I.I.T. is here. Got shots so S.Q. tomorrow

June 30 Saturday
S.Q. all day. Read another book. Went to Manistee in Garvers truck & helped in shipping.
Drover somewhat. Ran off more pages of the "Acumln" tonight and played more pool.

July 1st Sunday
Went to church at the 1st Cong. Church in Manistee today. Had a good but small worship service. Read & played ball this afternoon with discussions at 7:00. Long talk with Alfred Ames from I.I.T. in Chicago & knew Don Hayakawa & Koryapiski** well. Interesting character. Am dead broke as I gave $2.00 to co-op stores.

July 2nd Monday
Worked in the kitchen today from 12:30 to 8:00 P.M. Hard work—dead feet but interesting.

** *Eddy was in noteworthy company, Alfred Ames was a teacher at the Illinois Institute of Technology (ITT) Ames, who later wrote for the Chicago Tribune, was credited by James Alfred Wight, who wrote under the name of James Herriot in 1972, for making his writing career a success after a rave review of Herriot's "All Creatures Great and Small".*

Don Hayakawa, also known as S.I Hayakawa, was also at ITT at the time. Hayakawa later became a well-known California Senator.

Koryapiski was actually Alfred Korzybski, a Polish-born independent scholar who was instrumental in the study of general semantics. Eddy likely knew them all them from his time with the cooperative movement in Chicago.

July 3

Cleaned totally—last dorm. This morning discussion classes, this afternoon girl here who's hair reminds me of Fran's. Her husband plays pool with us and every time I see the back of her head, I miss my shot. She's about the same size and build which makes it even harder to pass off. She is leaving this weekend so maybe I'll forget it. In a way I'm glad she's leaving cause it makes me awfully darned homesick.

Through the grace of God, I've fallen in with Roscoe Swank. He is older than I am, as near perfect example as I could have. We bunk next door & have built a writing -desk-shelves.

Combination is swell. I'm beginning to feel the change in me already. Should we say of Religious Courage? It's not yet where I want it but it's coming!!!!!

July 4

Work today was nil because of a morning of rain showers. Afternoon we had a 4th of July baseball game which ended 9-7. It was topped off by a beautiful draped table of a banquet. With the after dinner speech arx oll.†† Only after effect so far is a splitting headache which may last a week.

July 5

Flub dubbed. Went to Hogshack and fell down. Second orientation

July 6

Went to extension mowed away and along the creek there. Out to Commoners pine plantation about 12 years old.

---

†† *No idea what "arx oll" is or means but with the headache that followed, it was evidently too much for a 19 year old non-drinker to handle.*

July 7
Had the shots last night, leaving for camp[‡‡] this afternoon. Arrived 9:30 in the evening, no train

July 8
At camp Rode horseback, swam, friends meeting, discussion, hard time getting away— literally and figuratively. Swell weekend—but no Fran. Saw Mom and Dad

July 9   Monday
The fellows met me at Martin Mich. 2:30 A.M.[§§] rode to camp, swell trip all around. Fire training today, back pack pumps full of water are slightly heavy—anyway not light. Learned how they put fires out. Also how to detect them and learned to work the 2 way radio. Slept this evening.

July 10
Last night I slept for 13 hours straight, gosh was I tired! Went on the Baldwin crew for today. Cut the lawn at the ranger station there. Quite a job but really fun. In the afternoon we drove by where they had a big fire this spring.

July 11
Pulled me from Baldwin. Went to work in the kitchen crew. We are on the afternoon shift. Then are automatically on the tanker crew. Played baseball this evening, had a good game and plan to have more. Bed about 10:15

[‡‡] *When granted a weekend away from Wellston, Eddy headed off to Circle Pines. Workers were able to take time off away from the camp, but it was often more practical to remain at the camp because of financial restraints, and logistical problems going to and from a destination.*
[§§] *The 147 mile trip from Martin, MI. to Wellston was at least a two-and-a-half-hour trip. They rolled into Camp 42 after 5 in the morning, a good time to put the boys to work!*

July 12

Kitchen for good now. Fellow came in about transferring to Lyons New Jersey.*** Good idea and it would come after Youth Institute for C.S.C. Movie tonight was "Our hearts were young and gay"††† Good movie- best I've seen here yet.

July 13

Worked in the kitchen this afternoon. Wrote 5 letters and 3 postcards. Had loads of fun and had a baseball game this afternoon

July 14

Worked in kitchen this afternoon and piled up 4 camp hours.‡‡‡ Played pool last night.

July 15

Church in Manistee, dinner at camp, afternoon shift in kitchen, 4 camp hrs.

*** *Lyons was CPS Camp 80, located at Lyons, New Jersey. It was on the grounds of a mental hospital and the camp was run by the Brethren Service Committee. There were two parts to the camp, one dealt with the mental patients and the other was a veterans' hospital facility. A transfer could mean working at one, the other or both.*

Eddy did not mention why he was seeking a transfer but when he spoke with someone about Lyons, he came away thinking this might be a better position for him. Perhaps someone had stories of a better service elsewhere or the strain he had known before his arrival may have still been prevalent. He was accustomed to kitchen work, but the prospect of not just months but of perhaps years of kitchen labor spurred him to find anything else.

††† *CSC may be a reference to "Civil Service Commission" "Our hearts were Young and Gay" had been released the previous year. It featured the comical misadventures of two young women on a ship bound for Europe. Directed by Lewis Allen, it starred Gail Russell, Diane Lynn and Charles Ruggles.*

‡‡‡ *July 14 and 15 were the weekend, he logged extra work time for his work in the kitchen.*

100

July 16
Kitchen 12 hours today, went to Ludington and saw Diamond Horseshoe[§§§] also two other comedies Got home about 4:05

July 17
Slept till 12:00, played piano also tried "Sentimental Journey"

July 18
Slept later than usual, played piano & read. Afternoon crew kitchen

July 19
Movies tonight, on birds first and Inca Indians. Started a knife for Fran, I still love her but she'll never believe me again.[****] Got radio in box of things today but no tubes. Played bridge till 11:45 PM

July 20
Worked on knife in morning. Aft. Shift Tubes came in today, also good clothes. Have radio on now. Excellent reception.

July 27
Picked cherries[††††] today after morning of work

[§§§] *Diamond Horseshoe was a Betty Grable and Dick Haymes film about a medical student who wants to sing in a nightclub and the beautiful showgirl who is asked to dissuade him.*
[****] *Eddy's first reference to problems with Fran. Whatever the problem was, it had been serious enough for Fran to throw a ring he'd given her into Stewart Lake.*
[††††] *The upper part of the lower peninsula of Michigan is known for its cherry crop. The weather along the shores of Lake Michigan and carrying inland provides the right microclimate for the fruit crop. COs had the opportunity to earn cash by putting in extra time harvesting fruit.*

Cherries have an extremely short season and are very weather sensitive. Normally, harvest is completed in under a month, but the season can last seven or eight weeks, from the first week of July till the end of August.

101

July 28 Sat.
Worked in bake shop from 4:30 A.M. to 4:00 P.M. Flat as heck.

July 29 Sunday
Worked afternoon shift in kitchen today. Next week hope to go to Interlochen.‡‡‡‡ Check on my Inst. At C.P.C. So far OK, need OK from Elgin on Lyons transfer, swell.

July 30
Worked on knife in morning. Benn loafing too much, must stop if ever expect to have Fran.
Brought diary up to date today. Wrote several letters.

July 31
Worked on morning shift today. Cherry picking $3 earned all afternoon and eve.§§§§ Home in bed by 10:15

Aug 1
Morning shift again Cherry picking this afternoon $5

Aug 2
Cherry picking netted $6.00 today

The Wellston area local farmers were glad to enlist the assistance of workers from camp 42 when they could. Workers were in short supply. The crops wait for no one.

‡‡‡‡ *Interlochen is a world-renowned arts camp and institute an hour north of Wellston. It was established in 1928, 10 years before Circle Pines. There was a natural interest in another facility that mirrored many programs similar to CPC.*

§§§§ *Cherry picking provided a small influx of cash. From the stories of unrest before Eddy arrived at Wellston, Camp 42, it's unclear if any wages were being paid to the COs. Some of the peace churches provided some funds for COs but their government work was unpaid. Even though it was to be considered "work of national importance," many viewed it more as a prison release work crew.*

Aug 3
Stayed home today, not much but played piano and slept.

Aug 5
Worked 1 ½ shifts today, kept quite busy. Am very tired. Had an accident last night which has troubled me all day. Must be more careful because of my rupture.*****

***** *Eddy's "accident" and unexplained rupture notwithstanding, before any approval for a transfer could appear, another opportunity came up. A new program was being tested in which CPS workers would transfer over to the United States Forest Service. They were looking for volunteers. Eddy along with 5 other camp 42 workers jumped at the chance.*

Chapter 17
Wellston Part 2

C amp 42 workers had already received training in many of the jobs the US Forest Service was looking for, though the direct training Eddy had received was sparse, as he was shuffled from one job to the next. Most of the learning was to come from doing. The USFS was putting together a small mobile squad for work in the southern part of the United States.

The US Forest Service was an important cog in the inner workings of maintaining the country. Wood was such a vital resource during both war and peace time, and the Forest Service was tasked with maintaining both the nationally held lands and large timber stands held by private concerns. The image of the service was also under re-branding.

The previous year, the USFS and the War Advertising Council had introduced the fictitious "Smokey the Bear" as their mascot for fire prevention.[*] The first poster with Smokey appeared in 1945.

The Forest Service was responsible for managing so many different tasks. Because of the war it was dealing with the manpower shortage for fighting fires. It was trying to establish the "smoke jumpers," who parachuted into remote locations for firefighting and protection. It was charged with managing the grazing of cattle on government owned ranges and dealing with the cattle barons who had contracted for use of the

---

[*] *The true story we know about a badly burned young bear cub as the only survivor of a New Mexico forest fire did not happen till 1950. The cub was named Smokey, after the bear in the campaign and moved to the National Zoo in Washington D.C., where he lived till his death in 1976.*

property, it was also responsible for overseeing the cleanup and salvage from a hurricane that had swept the New England coast in 1938, leaving millions of damaged trees in danger of fire and insect infestation.[†]

Along the west coast, women were hired in to help in the watchtowers, one of the first lines of defense against an invasion. The Forest Service also established crews to plant and reforest previously damaged or harvested timber lands, all the while overseeing our national forests for both preservation and what was in the best interest for the nation.

This was a very different type of service compared to Eddy's first two months. His unit traveled and worked in the South, covering the states of Mississippi, Louisiana, Arkansas, Texas, Oklahoma, Alabama, and Florida. While there were facilities they could use, being a mobile unit also meant they set up rural base camps as they moved from state to state.

Little is known about the men he traveled with or how much additional service regular Forest Service employees provided, but Eddy was an experienced outdoor camper. He knew how to start fires, how to cook over an open flame, how to pitch a tent, how to use a forest toilet.

What his time in the Forest Service taught him was a protocol—an order to both how and where a new camp was to be set.

First things first: find what would be the main gathering point, preferably a flat area with plenty of space. Find an area with trees, then suspend ropes from several to form a triangle or small square and use tarps to create a roof. This "dining fly" became a makeshift room in which the men prepared and ate food, and, in the case of rain, it protected them and their gear.

They may have had tents for locations where they stayed longer, but the dining fly was desirable for an open-air kitchen

---

[†] *In all, over a three-year period, they were able to direct the salvage of over 700 million board feet of timber.*

and gathering space. The end of summer into early fall can be quite hot in the South and there is always a need for shelter from both the sun and rain. Besides establishing a dining structure or "fly" area, they needed to secure a potable water source and an outdoor latrine. Personal sleeping areas were set up, along with all other areas required for a functioning camp. With his experience, Eddy was comfortable taking charge and he had a willingness to muster and direct help. He had the ability to see in his mind what the finished base camp should look like and direct those around him to make it happen.

This was a unique situation. The men were not in the military, so there wasn't a set chain of command. The Forest Service may have been their boss, but it's unclear what type of dominion it had over the workers. The workers likely honored the job requests to fulfill their work of national importance because they were men who had become CO's from having high moral convictions, but they weren't going to stand for being taken advantage of or being abused. The job itself most closely resembled the work of timber cruisers. They had received a minimal amount of training as cruisers before they came to the Forest Service. Their jobs included mapping out parcels of forest land and recording a sampling of the number of trees, identifying each species, noting their maturity level by the size of their girth and height, and determining availability in case the timber was necessary for a national emergency.

Unlike the military, there was no government issue clothing when Eddy and the men he worked with showed up to the CPS camps. There was no daily required uniform. For the most part, men were supported by their families and the peace churches, but the Forest Service had special equipment that the men needed for their work in the woods. This included leather climbing boots that were laced up to just below the knee, providing a sense of security from the occasional snake bite. Those boots facilitated the use of climbing spikes, a necessary hardware item for scaling the trees. Not everyone was cut out for scaling, but it was a job Eddy took on.

Though the primary work of these special crews were timber cruisers and surveyors, Eddy's view of why he was traveling the poor, rural South (a view shared by other crews doing similar work in other parts of the country) was a bit different. He believed that a sizeable part of their work was to find ways to help and to provide education.

Most, if not all, of the men were very spiritual, and they believed that they were to perform in some religious capacity. One man from another camp who was doing similar work in the East said, "While the camp remained, many of the men grew increasingly frustrated with the need to perform menial work. They held high hopes for using their training and experience in teaching, rural rehabilitation, community organization, religious work more directly in areas of high need."

This begs the question of how the program was presented by the Forest Service to the COs and what was said to motivate them to volunteer. Perhaps there was more to the offer, and for men of great conviction, the desire to do good Samaritan work—work which to them was the opposite of going into an area and killing people— was the equivalent of a moral victory. Even if the Forest Service had people who thought that providing assistance to an impoverished area was a good thing, there were some others in the government who thought just the opposite. There were those in the Selective Service who did not want pacifists spreading their "propaganda." These people did not want COs to be allowed to freely mingle with local populations and gain acceptance. What if others could be persuaded that war and service in the armed forces was not a good and honorable thing?

One of the more interesting aspects of the interplay between the Forest Service, government and the CO's was that there was another reality, that of the people who lived where the COs were working. Eddy's discovered that, by and large, there was a huge distrust of the government in the rural area. While working in the large woodlots, following backroads and old timber trails far away from main roads, the COs had a real fear of being attacked and killed. Some of the locals looked at them as spies, sent by the government to seek out moonshine and stills. Out in the woods, away from civilization, was ideal for setting up a hidden distillery. High up in a tree, a man had a better vantage point from which to spot illegal activity. You cannot distill moonshine without a fire. Where there is fire, there is smoke, and the men were trained to spot smoke and to be able to make educated guesses as to its origin. There was some discussion as to whether they needed to go the woods armed, a tough position for the Objectors to be in.

The forests where they worked, whether nationally held or one of the large publicly held lots, were a great national treasure. The men knew their work was one of treating the woods with respect, of trying to preserve and improve it. Regardless of their disappointment in failing to connect with the local population, they knew their work mattered.

WW II had officially ended on September 2, 1945, but Eddy and the other men were fulfilling their duty to the country and continued to work in the Civilian Public Service Corp and the Forest Service even though peace was declared. The terms of service were not well defined, and most of the discharges from the CPSC occurred well after peace had been declared. Even with all the distractions of the work at hand, Eddy's thoughts never strayed far from home. He not only longed for a time when he could return, but there were issues plaguing Circle Pines that caused him concern. Away from home, he was able to reflect on what he saw as important.

Everett and Viola sat on the Board of Directors and kept him informed about how the camp, farm, and folk school at Circle Pines were interacting. The farm was expanding and, while there was a grand plan for what the folk school could become, the camp was at the heart of where they had started.

On Oct. 18, 1945, Eddy wrote from Tallulah, Louisiana. He may have written the letter just for himself but a copy of it was more than likely shared with Fran, because in March of 1946, Eugene Dungan, Fran's father, shared Eddy's thoughts with every member of Circle Pines:

Our car drove us down the long gravel road, pines on both sides of us, and a low rustic building before us. We were there. Once again we had come to spend our summer vacation at Circle Pines Center. "Oh Look Mom" I cried, "There's Batt and Kap."

Yes, there were a lot of old friends there, and new ones too. There were a lot of memories from last year, our first and the camps first. I was young, about eleven or twelve, and certain things I remember very clearly.

I remember that here kids my age could folk dance with the older folks. We could attend recreation institute; we could play volleyball on the court with Pipp Baumann, Dick Bannasch, Murry Roth, Mike Lamont, Barney, and others. We could go to town and watch Jack Gordon play tennis. We could swim and learn to dive. We could walk through the woods.

We know that Bob Stockdale was always in his craft shop, willing to teach us the tricks of the lathe, and Dot Sonquist helping us with billfolds and moccasins, John Morgan with his Shepard's pipes, Dave with his stories of the stars on star-gazing hill, Kap and the way he played "The road to Madalay," the rolling bass in "lift every voice and sing," "Song Of Michigan," "Hymn of the hills," "march of the youth," out of our dreams of living freedom," and "Evening prayer." The art sessions at the lake front. The food of Ma Panzner and Bill Jones.

"What's that they're talking about? A new camp? What wrong with this one?"

"Oh I see, the Government owns it and we're never sure if we can rent it or not.

Where? About seven miles from here? Fine!"

Yes—a new camp, and a swell lake. An old farm. "A

work camp? Swell idea, at the lake? Wonderful! Hey, there's Doc Wildman, Hi Doc! And Harry Wolfe, Doctor Strauss, Ruth Kurtz, Kap! Ted Teal, Dave—Gosh, the same old gang."

Yes—they were all here, the same old gang; Mike and barney, Murry, Jack, Pipp and Dick B., and we danced. Almost as much as before

> We're building a camp!

And we were happy.

And we played volley ball.

> Two games in several years "but we're building a camp!

And we were satisfied.

And they played tennis

Once or twice

But we're building a camp!

And we worked

"A farm? Sure, you must have food to feed the campers, Hey! That's swell! Fresh vegetables on camp tables. A farm—swell! And horses, cows, pigs and even chickens too."

"A folk school—gosh that's good; we can study and work at the same time.

Wonderful!"

"A community? Sure—Wait a minute. They're good ideas, but lets see now... how far back? Community? NO. Folk school? Oh—no. Farm—is that it? No. Oh yes, a summer camp! What ever happened to our institutes on recreation?

"Hey! Murry, Pipp, Fred, Mike! How about a game of volleyball?" "craft teacher, how about teaching us to run the lathe? To the eyes of an eleven-year-old these things are strange. Five years to a thirteen-year-old makes him eighteen. That's a long time to miss these things.

"But we're building a camp"

And we argued

To me, that young boy, Circle Pines has one clear aim; that of serving this nation with a new kind of recreation—one where children, youth, and adults of all races and creeds can get together, and live together, work together, study together, learn together, and play together. Our first step must be a step in which we can have the largest group of people doing these things simultaneously. This can only be done by a camp— where hundreds can enjoy the breeze on "star hill," the morning dips, the skits, volleyball, baseball, and folk dancing.

With this goes the farm, an important part in the feeding of hungry campers. Last but far from least comes the folk school and community. Community and folk school— these are projects in which fairly few people may partake. These, therefore, must be secondary.

How long will it be before we have a camp? If twenty years, one fourth of it is already gone and we aren't building a camp. But some time once again, when that eleven-year-old is twenty-one…or thirty…or forty, he will play volleyball with the youngsters, and then we will say,

"But we built this camp!"

And we will be at ease.

Sincerely,

Everett Edwards jr.

Eddy understood how a simple idea had very quickly become very complex. Circle Pines was his refuge, and while a thousand miles from home, and no doubt a bit homesick, he knew what he wanted it to be. Not that all the proposed side ventures to him didn't have merit, but he wanted those who now followed to have the same impact on them as his camping experience had had on him. The folk school was at the center of his education, while the farm drove the need to provide food and shelter. It was the camp that surrounded his soul.

111

Soon it was time to return to the forests of Michigan. By the time the men moved back north, winter had set in. Eddy had missed the glorious fall colors of the hardwood forests of mid-Michigan, the Christmas holiday had come and gone, and a new year had arrived. Eddy returned to Wellston on January 2, 1946. He had only known the camp during the summer months. Now, with the cold and snow, the day-to-day routine was very different.

For the crews at the camps, meals still needed to be provided three times a day. But in the winter, it was also necessary to gather wood for heating fires.

As part of the strategy of working the men, Wellston had a workshop where they could pursue craft projects making rugs, ceramics, woodworking, and leather work, but part of their time was spent in a commercial venture group, producing items such as children's wood toys and wooden kitchen items. Many of the men found great joy in the work which they could share with the local population.

Eddy remained at Wellston until the camp closed in September of 1946. Then he and the other workers were assigned to other camps throughout the United States.

Chapter 18
Beyond Wellston

After Wellston, Eddy relocated to Camp 34, a fish and wildlife-based camp located in Bowie Maryland. He never mentioned if any of the other men he was stationed with were transferred with him.

The camp was located on the Patuxent Wildlife Refuge, a short distance outside of Baltimore, Maryland. As a research station, their focus was on doing special projects for the Department of Agriculture and Interior.

Camp 42 had been run by the Mennonites and Eddy always spoke of his overall experience at 42 in glowing terms.

While Camp 34 also had the Mennonites listed as their administrators, it was jointly run by the Brethren Service Committee and The American Friends Service Committee. By the time Eddy arrived, the camp was being managed by the Brethren. Eddy's description of the camp: "rotten food, poor administration, few facilities, small staff, all put together means a continuous struggle."

This assessment of Camp 34 appears to be accurate and not just the musings of an unhappy 19-year-old. While the history of Patuxent Wildlife refuge area was long, going back to the Revolutionary War era, the weight of maintaining a facility that had only recently been established by Franklin D. Roosevelt in 1936 had taken its toll.

Research was taking place, but those in charge encountered difficulties in trying to run a facility while not only building the infrastructure, but also trying to do so during war time. During the war years the refuge administrators were trying to update, renovate, and build buildings. They were also tasked with many projects in creating what was to be a park and wildlife refuge. Roadways needed to be built and maintained. Ponds needed to be dug and stocked with fish. The CO's provided the work force. Materials and tools to do the jobs were in short supply and hard to come by. Nothing was easy.

Even after the war, the CO work force was constantly changing and there was an ongoing issue of matching the COs to a fitting job. Many of the Objectors held college degrees, but an ongoing complaint from all the camps was the under-utilization of the talent pool they had. Often, the work of the CO was labor-intensive grunt work.

There was an overall attempt to make the camp as self-sufficient as possible. For the men who came from a farming background, there was field and agricultural work. Some of the farm work was an effort to make up food shortages in Objectors families. They worked to provide both fruits and vegetables, along with fresh meat from hogs they raised.

With plentiful farm work available, along with the agricultural skills most had acquired working in rural areas, the other needs—carpentry, mechanical skills to work on machinery, general janitorial services, and maintenance jobs throughout the camp—were hard to staff. There was a continual scramble to meet the needs of the camp, and it started long before Eddy arrived.

During 1943, a project for additional staff residences had plans submitted and approved. Though it was given a priority rating, and a plan to use CO labor, along with wood milled on site, the Selective Service denied funding, so the project was delayed and then abandoned. At one point when the occupancy of the COs jumped from 50 to 70, makeshift additional dormitory housing had to be converted from other buildings.

Around the same time, another National Park Service camp, Camp Patapsco, closed. Much of the equipment, materials, and tools from Camp Patapsco were transferred to Patuxent. It was up to the workers from Camp 34 to rehabilitate buildings to store additional supplies.

Building projects were ongoing, but by the time the war ended, labor shortages and weather had created significant problems. Several times there were significant reductions of Objectors at the camp due to reassignments. July of 1945, Maryland set an all-time record for rain—almost twice the normal amount. Much of the labor was assigned to repairing damage caused by excessive water. With the continuous decline of Objector labor, manning the farm became almost impossible. There was barely enough labor to do essential maintenance and operations.

Despite labor issues and excessive rain notwithstanding, there was a push to move forward on the projects at the refuge. For an exchange of funds from the Army Engineers, they were able to acquire extra equipment: a bulldozer, grader, and dragline crane. There also was an opportunity to move the camp to a Civilian Conservation Corp facility in Beltsville when the buildings there were vacated by the Army Engineers.

When Eddy arrived, essential items were being transferred from a camp in Virginia for setting up a usable facility. The only project listed for that fiscal year was the construction of a dam on Snowden Creek. Work started in July of 1946, but often was stalled from a combination of lack of repair parts for broken machinery for and insufficient manpower. Furthermore, the Selective Service had begun a point system for discharging CO assignees, which took a toll on available labor.

Eddy spent most of his working hours in the office. For a newcomer to Camp 34, his job more than likely was non-essential, requiring no special skills or training. He could have been better suited to working in the kitchen as he had done at Camp 42, but perhaps he was tired of cooking. He complained about the food, but the camp had to transition from the time when they were able to provide much of their own food. Now they had to rely on government-provided supplies.

During his free time, Eddy enrolled in a local night school program. He took a class in comparative religion, which he thought was terrific. It was a time of personal introspection during which he realized that returning to school presented some significant problems. As Fall arrived, the Brethren Church no longer had the financial resources to manage the camp. On December 10, 1946, the Brethren transferred Camp 34 to government control. On the same day, Eddy was given his discharge papers signed by Lewis Kosch, Colonel, field artillery, US Army, who was listed as Assistant Director, camp operations and Duane H. Ramsey, Camp Director.

Eddy was 5'8" and 187 pounds at the time of his discharge. Even though his eyes were very blue, they listed his eye color as gray. He was issued three bus tokens which took him from Laurel, Maryland to Hinsdale, Illinois via Safeway Trailways and Illinois Greyhound Lines. He was also given a meal ticket which was good for one meal at each meal stop made by the bus lines, not to exceed one dollar.

Eddy's time in the Civilian Public Service was complete. He had served one year, five months and twenty days and was headed home in time for Christmas.

Chapter 19
Released from duty

E ddy arrived home with no money in his pocket. No parades or welcome home signs greeted him. No G.I. Bill provided for services since his discharge. But Eddy was never bitter. He also wasn't anti-military or anti-government. He had served his country honorably as a Conscientious Objector in the Civilian Public Service. His brother had done the same, as had their new brother-in-law, Barney, a fellow Conscientious Objector who had met Dorothy while serving in Chicago.

Eddy served the least amount of time of the three men. He was not only the youngest, but World War II had drawn to a close. The need for draftees was quickly changing.

The results of the objector program were mixed. Eddy found out later that someone in government had objected to his discharge. Some in power sought to punish anyone who applied for objector status. It was argued that COs should not be seen as noble or honorable.

This might be why Eddy's battle with the draft board and subsequent serving in the Civilian Public Service Corp should have ended with his discharge, but it didn't.

During the war years, approximately 43,000 men filed for objector status. Less than a quarter of them were classified 4-E. There were 4,872 others who, like Bruce, were sentenced to prison for a total sentence period of 12,000 years. Some were allowed to serve in non-combat roles, evidently at the discretion of various draft boards, with medics and chaplains being two of the more common non-combat positions.

Though the work of national importance was seen by some as a ploy to give these men something to do while not serving in the Armed Forces, there was a severe manpower shortage, and the service of COs can't be ignored. They volunteered for many medical experiments allowing the government to abuse them in the name of science. They were "human guinea pigs" testing the effects of medicines and pesticides, and human endurance, pushing the limits of what the body could endure. They even volunteered for studies to evaluate the physiological and psychological effects of near starvation.

Some of the COs who tired of being seen as draft dodgers and as cowards were motivated to take on the more dangerous jobs. For some it was necessary to prove themselves to family, friends, and general public. Whether it was fighting forest fires as smokejumpers or volunteering as experiments in human starvation, they put their bodies on the line.

As a whole, the men who served in Civilian Public Service generally found the experience to be a positive one.

"I had learned many different types of work and learned new skills," Eddy said, "I had increased my fund of knowledge many fold."

However, it was also acknowledged that often the work they performed was not as significant as they had been led to believe. By the end of 1944, the COs had completed almost 5,000,000 man-days of labor. All for no pay. If calculated at the Army rate of pay of $50.00 per month, the value of their work was more than $10,600,000. The churches bore the cost of maintaining and administrating the objectors and by the end of the war, found their own resources had been stretched to the limit.

The analysis of the work performed by the American Friends Service Committee after the program ended found that the utilization of the men was poor at best. Much of the work, even though it was of great help to the country, could have been postponed till after the war. There was a feeling that much of the work was based upon the Civilian Conservation Corp, which had been established to provide work for young men with no professional training and limited experience—a significant contrast to the CPS, which bore a large number of college educated men.

Misplaced, under-utilized workers were common. In 1943, a physicist and authority on microscopy was assigned to clear trails for a year. A public heath engineer was pulling weeds in a nursery. A statistician was keeping records at a weather station. Many requested a change of service to something more suitable to their education, but were denied.

Meanwhile, agencies all across the nation were requesting help, but the Selective Service ruled that COs could only work for government agencies. The selection of the work was at the discretion of the Selective Service director. There were no restrictions to keep them from working in the public sector, but the assignments didn't happen. Perhaps this was done to encourage the public to see the program as a failure. A large part of the public already viewed the COs with contempt, and as criminals, slackers, and cowards.

In addition to the government's lack of leadership, the COs were typically perceived as an unpaid source of forced labor, not much different than slaves or convicts. Very little respect was shown to the men. The AFSC and the churches involved were able to provide some financial support to help the men with their basic needs for hygiene, and clothing. There were occasional opportunities, such as the time Eddy picked cherries, during which the men could earn extra money, but most relied on gifts and support from home.

One third of the COs were married and another third had dependent children. Had they been in the armed forces, they would have been eligible for assistance, but serving their country in the Civilian Public Service, they did not qualify for this aid. The AFSC did what it could to provide help for those families, but it had much more limited resources. No provisions were made if a man became injured and no benefits paid if he died while in the service.

Conscientious Objectors to war can emerge from any number of sources. A person's conscience needs to be recognized. There have been provisions in US law for COs since colonial times. It wasn't until 1965 when the United States Supreme Court reached a verdict in United States v. Seeger that struck down the requirement that a CO must believe in a Supreme Being and their claim as a CO came from that belief, and again in 1970 that there was a recognition that a person's moral and ethical belief can be viewed the same as one's religious beliefs and it wasn't necessary to belong to a religious group to qualify to be a CO. By the war's end, the American Friends Service Committee had paid over $1,500,000 to administer the Civilian Public Service, which it had raised through donations—all for the defense of and recognition of conscience and the belief that for true religious freedom, one does not need membership in a particular church to qualify.

Chapter 20
Homeward bound

Eddy made it home just before the Christmas holiday of 1946. The last few years had been very stressful for the family, so any type of happy gathering would be a welcome relief.

At home, he met Dorothy's husband Bernard "Barney." Dorothy, having finished her education at the University of Wisconsin, had gone to work in the Chicago office of the American Friends Service Committee where she fell in love with Barney, who was finishing up his service in the Civilian Public Service. The CPS placement in Chicago was largely involved in helping with the work AFSC was doing with clothing drives to help war torn Europe. Though Eddy was happy to reunite with his family for Christmas, Bruce was not so fortunate. He had been released from Sandstone Prison in Minnesota after seven months and assigned to work at one of the CPS camps located at the University of Michigan hospital in Ann Arbor.

It was often standard practice to deny a 4-E draft classification on an appeal. Failure to report for induction resulted in a prison term, only to have the prison board re-classify the inmate as a 4-E Conscientious Objector then to parole them to a CO camp.

This was a huge source of frustration for those who were not able to gain CO status; they were often judged even more harshly than those who had.

Most of the reasons for denying an appeal for a 4-E classification were listed in a study quoted by the AFSC that came from the Office of the US Attorney General:

1) Admission by the men themselves of political or non-

religious grounds for their stand, leaving them outside the scope of the law, which recognizes only those who are opposed to the war by "reason of religious training or belief."

2) A restricted interpretation of the meaning of religious training and belief by draft and appeal boards which excluded a number of men who claimed a religious basis for their objection.

3) Apparent error of local appeal boards in judging the sincerity of a man's conviction.

4) Failure of the men, through ignorance or some other reason, to exercise the right to appeal after being denied 4-E status by their local boards. Many agreed that the procedure as implemented created a great waste of human resources, and wrongly branded many honest objectors as law breakers.

While at the U of M hospital, Bruce was able to restart his college career, and was admitted to the College of Literature, Science, and the Arts. The work at the hospital was important and having additional workers was appreciated, though a different opportunity arose.

With the war effort over, there was a new task at hand, one which involved the rebuilding of Europe. A massive non-military undertaking to provide economic assistance to the European nations had begun.

Even before the end of World War II, a rebuilding plan was underway. In a conference of 44 nations, the United Nations Relief and Rehabilitation Administration (UNRRA) was formed to assist those countries that would eventually come under Allied control. Part of the plan came from an idea that came from Dan West while working in Spain as a relief worker after the Spanish Civil War. As a relief worker, West was charged with making the decision which children would receive rations of powdered milk and who would not, based on their rate of weight gain. He thought that it was a greater benefit to gift a cow to those in need rather than ration milk. "A cow, not a cup." From the birth of that idea came the refinement that a gift of a pregnant heifer, instead of cow who was already producing milk, allowed for the recipient to "pass on the gift" of the first female offspring. Implementation could not happen till after the war but the Heifers for Relief Committee or the "Heifer Project" was ready at war's end.

Bruce became aware of the project and discovered that there was a huge manpower void to facilitate the shipment of livestock to Europe. But there were some problems. The work Bruce was doing at U of M was under the authority of the CPS and The Heifer Project was not under their jurisdiction. Furthermore, Congress was undecided about whether to allow COs to work for the Heifer Project. There was a bill prohibiting the release of any CPS worker for any reason as long as combat troops were deployed, so the Selective Service was forced to withdraw their plan to release 75 CPS workers to UNRRA.

However, some COs were able to move over to the Heifer Project without government approval or reprisal.

To be eligible, men must have been assigned to CPS on or before October 31, 1944, and served continuously therein since that date. Men who had 18 months service in CPS as of that date were eligible to apply for transfer to the Civilian Public Service Reserve. When they did so, each applicant had to include in his letter of request to Colonel Kosch a statement of willingness to make at least one trip to Europe on behalf of the Heifer Project prior to discharge from the Reserve.

Bruce packed his bag and left Ann Arbor.

Bruce reported for duty in New Windsor, CT. Upon arrival, his first task was to obtain seaman papers from the Coast Guard Station. To be a cattle tender for the Heifer Project, he needed to become a registered Merchant Marine. He also needed to pass a separate physical examination from the War Shipping Administration and obtain a passport.

There was a difference between this job and working in the

CPS. This job paid. There was a salary of $150 per trip whether the trip took 6 weeks or 4 months. To make peace with the Merchant Marine union, which had no interest in having cattle tenders, the men were to be paid one cent a week to make them legally members of the Merchant Marines. All men were required to pay their own transportation home at the time of their discharge.

It was known as Camp 152, but it was not a CPS camp. The workers were known as the Seagoing Cowboys and the project unofficially called the "cattle boats."

According to a 1946 bulletin, livestock attendants (cattle boat workers) were required to feed, water, and care for approximately 25 animals apiece. During the time at sea, the men were under the legal authority of the captain of the ship. When ashore, they were under the control of UNRRA. Between June of 1945 and the early months of 1947, 7000 seagoing cowboys provided the manpower to deliver livestock to Europe. Of those, 366 were from CPS.

While Bruce had shared many years with Eddy at Circle Pines, he had not spent as much time working with elements of the farm. This was to become a family joke. Barney quipped that the one who grew up on a farm working with animals was in Chicago shuffling papers while the one who grew up in the city was on a boat tending to livestock.

A letter dated May 4, 1944, from a worker on one of the ships provided a glimpse of the daily work.

> We left Norfolk Mar 20, loaded with 375 heifers & tons of jam and peanut butter. (Arrived back in Baltimore, May 1st) With the exception of the first three days, the work was fairly easy. The schedule was something like this: up at 7:00 A.M.—feed cows chop (i.e. mixture of soy meal & cotton seed) Breakfast 7:30—feed cows hay and water, then haul up fresh hay, straw, and chop from hold with block and tackle. This was usually done by 10:30 or 11:00. Lunch at 11:30. In the afternoon we have to start work 2:30 or 3 depending

on how long it took us to rake the manure out of our cows' stalls, bed them with straw, feed chop—hay & water. Sometimes we had to come back after supper and work till 6 or 6:30. However we did not throw the manure overboard nor thoroughly clean the stalls until we got into port. On some ships this is done daily and is considerably harder.

Of the 7000 seagoing cowboys, ages ranged from 19 to 33, only two men made four trips, 18 made three, and 91 made two. All the rest made one trip. Bruce was one of the 18, making three voyages to Europe and back.

Starting on July 11, 1946, Bruce served on the SS Frederick C. Howe, going from Newport News to Czechoslovakia. They carried 707 horses, but unfortunately, 42 horses died at sea.

For his second trip, he was promoted and served as foreman which included an increase in pay to $250 for the trip on the SS Queens Victory carrying 770 horses to Poland. This time they lost only 8 animals.

His final trip left Newport News on the SS Zona Gale on November 11, 1946. Once again he served as a Foreman Cattle Attendant, heading out again with a load of 373 horses for Czechoslovakia. During this trip there was a devastating storm and they lost 45 horses.

Returning to home port in the early part of 1947, Bruce found his own way back to Ann Arbor to finish out his term of service and discharge from CPS.

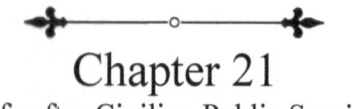

Chapter 21
Life after Civilian Public Service

In January, 1947, while Bruce was at sea, Eddy headed into the city where he found work again with the National Co-operative. This time he worked with the accounting department.

In his free time, he began to do educational work with a high school youth group who were following the co-operative movement. This led to involvement in several conferences and committees. He looked for opportunities to start in a higher education program, but his busy schedule allowed for little extra time for schooling.

Circle Pines was still very much at the forefront of his mind. Everett and Viola had worked on the board of directors, and the family remained engaged with the growing center, it was also a place of much internal turmoil. The grand plans of building a folk school had met with resistance from some of the members of the Circle Pines co-operative. Trying to find a way to make all the different pieces fit together and work to sustain the facility was problematic.

There were many who were not in favor of the push to construct the buildings for which Frank Lloyd Wright had provided drawings. The cost of the buildings was considerable. Since Wright was involved, there was an agreement on how he was to be paid in conjunction with the construction of any of his plans. There was no good way to fund the project without going to the membership.

Some members saw the need to separate out different entities: the camp, the school, the conference center, the farm, and an area for industry. They envisioned a contained community. Many others focused on what had attracted them to Circle Pines—the opportunity for inexpensive recreation with likeminded cooperators. The other concepts, while they might make Circle Pines more financially feasible, were not very appealing to that part of their clientele. For Eddy, the carefree days he shared with Fran at the Center had passed. There wasn't the same draw for him as when he left for public service. While not in attendance, he was voted to Circle Pines' board of directors, so he remained engaged with the camp. By the time summer rolled around, a spot opened up in the purchasing department of the National Co-operative and Eddy moved into what he saw as a better job fit.

Eddy lived at the family home while working in the city. His grandmother, who was semi-invalid and required a full-time nurse, came to live with them. The family was under considerable financial strain, but as long as Eddy stayed working, he carried his share of the load.

In the summer of '47, Everett Sr. found new employment and with it a significant increase in pay. Eddy took the opportunity to seek higher education.

His search for schools took him to Oskaloosa, Iowa, and William Penn College, a Quaker college. Perhaps his brother-in-law Barney, who briefly attended there, or Fran's father Eugene, who had also attended, influenced this decision. In any case, now considering himself more aligned with the Quaker religion, Eddy quickly fell in love with the school.

He headed west on a five-hour drive to make Oskaloosa his new home. Oskaloosa was slightly larger than Hinsdale, with a population of just over 11,000, but Hinsdale was outside of Chicago with many other suburbs next door. Oskaloosa felt much more like a small rural city to Eddy.

William Penn College was a small college. It had been shrinking in enrollment in the years leading up to World War II, but at war's end, the total student enrollment was close to one hundred.

Only two years earlier, in 1945, the first men's dorm had been added on campus. Before then, the men did not have on-campus housing and sought housing in town, boarding with residents. The female students did have dorms, where they could remain under the watchful eye of the administration. Off-campus housing for them was either to be in their own home, or by permission of the dean, they could live in the home of a faculty member or close family relative.

Campus life was a bit of a challenge for Eddy. He was no stranger to living in a group housing situation, but he was also starting college having gained much life experience. No longer fresh out of high school, he was older than many of his fellow students in the freshman class.

The student handbook dictated: "You will observe the customs of the college, which include refraining from smoking, drinking, and social dancing on the campus." Eddy neither smoked or drank, but there was the bounce of a dance in every step he took.

Upon starting at William Penn, one of his first tasks was to write an autobiography. Eddy titled his "It's been fun so far." On September 14, 1947, in the final paragraphs of his essay, he wrote:

> I came here, instantly liked it, took among other courses orientation, and had to write an autobiography and here it is.
>
> You will notice that I have left out three major fields of thought in this writing.
>
> Each one of these should be handled as a supplement as they are a story in themselves.
>
> One is, as you may have noticed, no girlfriends. The second is a very important one and that is my church life. I am a Congregational and Chairman of the local missionary action committee for three years. Seven years perfect Sunday school attendance. The third classification is one I feel I should do at a later date and that is our family. We have always had fun together and have developed a philosophy that is very easy to follow and that everyone appreciated equally well. If you would

like these, I will be willing to add them at a later date.

Eddy had no college credits which could be transferred. When he took classes while in the Civilian Public Service Corp, the courses were more of special interest to him, but he found the schooling difficult.

Penn had a music program in which he participated. There he quickly found himself a place, playing percussion in the orchestra. The orchestra had close to 25 members in it—nearly a quarter of the student population.

The student handbook mandated: "You will participate in all college activities. Study, work, worship, and recreation. Because you are part of the community, and you want to share in the whole community program. You will feel a concern for every other member of the community and will try to make friends with everyone."

Much of the inclusive nature of life at William Penn was what attracted Eddy to the college. It was a good fit for his belief system.

His first year at William Penn was uneventful. Finding friends was never a problem for him, nor was interjecting himself into the social scene. Like most students, he was destined to leave the college in the spring and seek out summer employment. Even with help from home, there was an expectation that he carried the burden of some of his finances.

Chapter 22
Pawling NY

As summer approached, Eddy was looking for an employment opportunity and, perhaps, something different. He came across a job located in Pawling, New York. A planned community surrounding a large lake in an area called Quaker Hill had an opening for a community lifeguard. As an older applicant, Eddy would be more desirable than someone just finishing their freshman year at college at age 18 or 19. He had spent the summer of '44 working as lifeguard, plus he brought a host of life experience and with it, one might expect more maturity to a job. It looked like a good fit for him.

Quaker Hill, however, was more than just a community swimming hole or local pool. Its history starts with Clover Brook Farm, on Quaker Hill Road in the town of Pawling. Half of the property was originally located in New York and the other half in Connecticut until the states could come to an agreement. In 1731, it was ceded to New York in exchange for other property which was then made part of Connecticut. Early residents of the farm, the Atkins family, dated back to 1741 and the family had a prominent position in the community. By 1863, after changing hands within the family, the property was upgraded with the construction of a new three story, 37 room, 8,448 square foot home featuring 9 bedrooms and massive stone fireplaces.

In 1926, while looking for property with easy access to New York City, broadcast journalist, author of "With Lawrence of Arabia" [*] (among others), and filmmaker, Lowell Thomas

---

[*] *Lowell Thomas both filmed and wrote about T.E. Lawrence, Lawrence of Arabia, which introduced Lawrence to the world leading to the popularity of his story and a later Hollywood film about his exploits.*

purchased the 500-acre farm for $33,000. Quickly, Thomas established a broadcast studio in the home. Because of both its size and its location, only 66 miles from New York City, he began to receive prominent guests at his home which included President Herbert Hoover, NY Governor Thomas Dewey, Edward R. Murrow, and Dr. Norman Vincent Peele. It was a place for the society crowd of NYC to come for a country visit.

Enjoying the serenity of the country life, Thomas bought an additional 3000-acre parcel from the estate of New York real estate developer Fred French to block any development. Whether by design or by natural progression, he began to parcel off some of his holding to friends so they could build and enjoy the rustic nature of the area away from the city. Among these friends were Dewey, Peele, Dr. Howard Rusk, and Elliot Bell.

As an enclave for his friends, the area was lacking in some of the refinements they had access to in the city. Thomas's solution was to add a community house, a golf course, and a ski slope. He was also instrumental in the choice of a clergyman to head the non-denominational church he attended when in town.

His property holdings included Lake Hammersley, which he renamed Quaker Lake. The lake was almost a mile long and surrounded by farm country with forests and rolling hills. Part of the reason the lake had never been developed is because the entirety of the lake had remained in the Hammersley family for 200 years, having been deeded to the family during the colonial days and the reign of Queen Anne. Although the name of the lake had changed, the ridge along its western shore is still known as Hammersley Hill. During the time that Fred French owned the property surrounding it, motorboats were forbidden from being used on the lake.

Thomas went on to develop Quaker Hills even further. As he parceled off everything from single lots to hundred-acre farms, it slowly became a planned community. A master landscape engineering study was done to assure they maintained a rural feel. An architect's committee oversaw the style of homes that could be built. Thomas himself kept a hand in the approval of families who were allowed to purchase land there. A real estate booklet noted:

"Lowell Thomas bought the entire lake and thousands of acres about it, re-named it Quaker Lakes and arranged for its settlement by additional desirable families."

With an eye on the social and recreational needs of his growing community, Thomas acted as host for regular Saturday evening parties and dances for the residents of Quaker Hill. At first, the parties were held in an old converted dairy barn, often with folk or hillbilly themes. Later, he constructed a newer community center. As part of the construction of the stone fireplace in the community center, he had stones from the Great Pyramid of Cheops, the Parthenon, St. Peter's Cathedral, China's Great Wall, and Mount Vernon installed.

In addition to golf and skiing, the large lake front made waterfront activities available.

Thomas was also a skilled horseman, so he made sure to establish more than 200 miles of bridle paths throughout Quaker Hill.

Eddy was no stranger to planned communities. In many ways, Circle Pines had been working continuously to become its own enclave of like-minded people. But where Circle Pines had prided itself as a place where all were welcome, where everyone's opinion mattered, and operations were a group decision, it lacked the scope of someone who could take the reins, finance the changes as they saw fit, and oversee the entire operation. Circle Pines provided an inexpensive place for a family vacation; Quaker Hills was where the powerful and wealthy of New York City went to play.

To Eddy's credit, he viewed all people equally. He didn't see a class difference or a need for exclusion, and in his eyes, that moral compass worked both ways.

Quaker Hills hired Eddy to work at the waterfront. The

boats were more magnificent than what he had to work with back at Stewart Lake and Circle Pines, but he also was there to work with the children. A natural leader of young people, he would rather spend time working with youngsters, improving their swimming strokes, than go out partying with a group of his peers. These were valuable traits to have when working under the watchful eye of someone like Thomas.

There were a host of other activities for Eddy to explore. He had spent enough time working on the farm at Circle Pines that he could be welcomed as a fellow farm worker. He had worked enough with the horses that he was comfortable around the animals. In addition to the things he knew about, there were some opportunities that were completely new, including the Quaker Hills' broadcast studio.

The electronic broadcast world was new and exciting as it expanded more into the public sector following World War II. New radio stations by the dozens were sprouting up across America. Eddy jumped at the chance to observe the studio in action, to speak with those who operated it.

Quaker Hills occupied a large portion of the Pawling countryside. Eddy had relied on public transportation to get him there, but it was going to take more than his feet to get from one part of the community to another. Thomas was kind enough to provide Eddy a 1943 Villiers Junior Motorcycle to use while in residence at Quaker Hill, though calling the machine a motorcycle was generous—it was little more than a scooter. Eddy was always more impressed with the Indian motorcycle over the Harleys, but the Villers was not in the same category as either.

Having been designed for the British military as something that could be airdropped behind enemy lines, the Villers was known as the paratrooper's scooter or Welbike, because it was designed to fit into a standard parachute container. Between 1942 and 1943, only 4000 were manufactured. In an effort to keep weight to a minimum, the bike was stripped down to the bare essentials. No suspension, no gears, no lights, and only one brake. It weighed 32kg. It is said that a paratrooper could unpack and have a Welbike running in 11 seconds. With a reported top speed of 30MPH, it was still better than walking the roads of Quaker Hill.

During the summer hoe-down themed parties, Lowell and his staff became aware of Eddy's love for folk dancing. They asked if he could act as the lead person for a folk or square-danced themed Saturday night party at the community pavilion while their usual caller took a night off. Of course, Eddy agreed.

This was to be a party like nothing he had attended before. It started with the decision that if he was to be the head square dance caller at a barn dance at Quaker Hills, he needed to look like the head square dance caller. Eddy was shuffled off to New York City where they found an outfitter to find him proper attire for what of the New York elite considered correct for a caller of square dances. He returned with a complete outfit: cowboy boots and hat, plaid flannel shirt, blue jeans with the legs cuffed, and a large belt buckle. He looked the part, in a Western sort of way.

Eddy was a natural at the speaking rhythm needed to be an effective caller. He was skilled at speaking in time while barking out instructions, singing his do-si-do's. He was neither afraid of public speaking nor public singing. As a trained percussionist, this was natural for him.

At the barn dance, Eddy was the center of attention. It was a thrill for him—one he never forgot. He spent the evening shaking hands and receiving pats on the back with words of praise and encouragement from the upper crust of New York. It was a world he had never before seen.

Though Eddy was the star of the barn dance, he wasn't always the darling of the Quaker Hills staff. One incident nearly cost him his job.

He had been politically active since his early high school days. He was knowledgeable and willing to politely debate his points of view. As many college students do, he loved to wear his political leanings on a tee-shirt. Had he been almost anywhere else, his "Truman for President" shirt was nothing more than clothing, but in Pawling—and especially at Quaker Hills—it was pointed out, in case he missed it, that Governor Thomas Dewey, the Republican nominee running against Truman, was a Quaker Hill resident. He, along with his family, all of whom Eddy had contact with, would certainly find the tee-shirt offensive.

While Eddy knew better than most that there is a time for your political voice and proclaiming your choice, free speech, and all of that, he recognized that this was not the time. He changed his shirt.

At some point during the summer, Eddy acquired a simple diving apparatus. Running off of an air compressor, he could wear a full-face mask, don flippers and a dive belt loaded with lead weights and do some close location diving. He became quite adept at diving this way. Because he was restricted by the length of his air hose, it wasn't the most efficient way to dive, but it was a new adventure, a new skill and a new way to go exploring. He packed up his apparatus and took it home with him at summers' end.

The summer ended too fast for Eddy. He had made friends and acquaintances whose names filled volumes. For all their fame, Eddy always felt like he was treated well. It left him with an overall sense of warm comradery for all of the residents he had contact with. For the rest of his life he considered the folks from Quaker Hill his friends.

Chapter 23
William Penn, Year Two

T he summer of 1948 was a very good summer for Eddy. By the end of August, Bruce had graduated with a bachelor's degree in economics from the University of Michigan. Eddy was the lone Edwards child still enrolled in college. In addition to earning a paycheck, he left Quaker Hills with a handful of new aspirations.

When September came, it was time to pack up his new-to-him wheels, a '37 Dodge coupe, with a couple of suitcases and an acoustic guitar and head back to school.

He had discovered that he was good at square dance calling. That might provide for some side income, if he could develop it, but in addition to that, at William Penn he saw an opportunity to learn about broadcasting. He changed his studies from the sociology path he had been following to a concentration on public speaking.

William Penn had a radio station that Eddy got involved with. He had spent time at Pawling developing a radio-style speaking voice. Perhaps it was just mimicking what he heard from Lowell Thomas, but it's also likely he was able to garner some professional critiques that showed him ways to improve.

The summer of '48 had signaled changes in the Selective Service. That June, a new Selective Service Act went into effect with the intent of modernizing the previous acts. Now every male between 18 and 25 years of age was eligible to be drafted for a service term of 21 months, followed by 12 months of continuous active service and then a term of 36 continuous months in the reserves.

This new Act included a 1-A-O classification for Conscientious Objectors to serve in non-combatant roles.

During the previous draft, the Selective Service had taken a general position not to grant non-combat service. Then when an objector appeared in front of his draft board, he was told, "You will be classified 1-A, you will carry a weapon and you will be required to fight."

The 4-E classification still was in use—one of 6 different classifications for objectors. 4E classification was listed just above 4-F, which was Unsuitable for Service.

The new Act had also added a 4-W classification for any objectors who had completed alternative service in lieu of induction.

Fall semester started much as expected for a sophomore college year, though plans for another school year of studies were constantly interrupted by extra-curricular activities.

One evening Eddy became involved in a memorable game of bridge. While in the Civilian Public Service, he had picked up several card games as a way to pass the time, but in this instance, when Eddy's partner realized he held a lay down grand slam and incorrectly bid the hand, in a fit, his partner upended the table sending cards and players flying. From that day on Eddy refused to play card games. He felt that if a game could enrage a player so much, it wasn't something he wished to participate in.

Just off campus was a supposed haunted house. Eddy and a group of his friends decided to get to the bottom of the myth. On Halloween, they entered the house with a single camera. There was a scream and then the flash of a flashbulb going off. They grabbed their equipment and ran.

Whitey, his friend who was named for a head of very light-colored hair, owned the camera—an old glass plate single-shot device. They had access to a darkroom on campus, so without wasting any time, Whitey went into the darkroom as the others waited outside for the results.

As moments passed, all they heard was a scream and the sound of breaking glass. Whitey was never able to tell them what he saw and remained mute, claiming no memory of the evening's activities. The proof they sought was lying in pieces on the darkroom floor.[†]

However, the sense of well-being that had carried Eddy from the summer into the fall was soon shattered. Eddy again faced a déjà vu moment as he faced the intrusion of the Selective Service back into his life.

Using the new draft law, on November 1, 1948, a notice was issued from Local Draft Board 121, in DuPage County that Everett Edwards Jr. had been classified 1-A, available to be drafted for military service.

This notice did not arrive at the Edwards' household in Hinsdale until November 6, though it appears Everett Sr. and Viola became aware of the new draft classification about the same time it was issued. It's possible that with all the time spent working with the draft boards, they had a friend who felt compelled to reach out to them about the decision to issue a 1-A classification. It's also possible that someone who was not in favor of the new classification alerted them. Bruce also received notice but since he was two years older was quickly approaching the cut-off age of 26.

On November 2, Viola was already receiving a reply from the National Service Board for Religious Objectors. Much like Eddy's earlier correspondence with the NSBRO, it outlined the procedures for appeal with the following at the end of the letter:

"The decision of whether to request an appeal or a personal appearance before the local board is one which he must make. Sometimes it is possible to obtain recognition of one conscientious objections from the local board in such a hearing. If the local board is antagonistic however, and he feels that his 1-A classification would not be changed, he may request an appeal directly. This will not prejudice his chances for

---

[†] *The story may not have been true, but it was great fun when Eddy told it.*

getting IV-E classification from the appeal board.

If the appeal board fails to sustain his claim for a IV-E classification he should notify our office immediately. If the decision of the appeal board is unanimous he has the right to request a presidential appeal within ten days following the notice of the appeal board decision. If the appeal board decision against him is unanimous it is still possible that the director of the Selective Service would take an appeal for him to the Presidential Appeal Board."

Yours Very Truly,
National Service Board of Religious Objectors
Signed,
Paul L Goering
Administrative Assistant

The letter from NSBRO was forwarded from home to Eddy at school. At the bottom of the letter, Everett attached a note:

Jr. Pls keep us informed of any reports, classifications, etc. you received. These things must be taken care of immediately when you receive them.

Dad

November 8, Eddy was ready with a response:

Dear sir,

I have received word from my folks that I have been classified 1-A by your draft board. I was under the impression that the classification would come after the form 150 was completed but find that obviously I was mistaken. You will find herewith the completed form you sent me, and an additional page of material.

If what I heard is correct and actual classification has been issued, and is 1-A, then I hereby wish to take this time to place on file my request for an appeal. As you will notice, if you are able to obtain my previous file, that during the first draft I was refused my classification till my file arrived in Washington where I was granted 4-E classification by the highest appeal board in the country, the presidential appeal board. I wish also to call attention at this time to the letters on file from the State Director of Selective Service and the letter from the Hearing Officer from the Northern District of Illinois.

In the future, please send all correspondence to me here at the college.

Yours,

Everett Edwards Jr.

As Eddy once again found himself faced with filling out government forms, now he included several notes about his life which were more current. From the additional sheets:

A good deal of my outside work has been with a group of high school students in the Chicago area. The name of the group was the Central States Co-operative Youth Council, of which I was first a member and then educational secretary.

It was through my Sunday school training under Rev. Ralph Douglas Hyslop that the foundation of my beliefs were laid and then through working in work camps under the auspices of the America Friends Service Committee (Quakers), that the entity of my beliefs were formulated.

I believe in the use of force, in the form of police protection but only to the point of where it means taking a life. In other words, I believe in the use of a restraining force, but definitely not to the point of killing.

During the first draft I served in a civilian Public Service camps for a period of more than 18 months. During this time, I volunteered for a special service in mental institutions and overseas which were refused because of physical reasons. Following this I requested and received transfer to a timber survey in the swamp area of Louisiana and the entire south, without any type of compensation.

I feel that through my entire service in Civilian Public

Service, I gave the continual expression of my beliefs and have always been willing to discuss the point whenever it has arisen. However, I feel that it is not proper to be antagonistic in my views, and therefore have not gone out of my way to project my views on other people.

I believe in a God of love. I believe that man was made to love, not to hate; to forgive, not to despise. I believe that wars and hatred are developed through the lust in the hearts and minds of men, for material things rather than that of action for service. I believe it is only through an undying faith in all men, and a sturdy love of God, that peace of any type will inherit the earth. I feel that the strong message of Jesus was that no manmade ruling, or lack of acceptance of a position, is at any time to supersede his message of love and therefore I find that I cannot rescind my position because of a human desire.

During the course of the last seven years, I have become increasingly interested in the Society of Friends (Quakers) Because of the lack of a meeting near our home I concentrated more along the lines of individual worship and meditation. Therefore, though I am still a Congregationalist by membership and still attend a Congregationalist church the majority of the time, I am in agreement more with the Friends than any other denomination. The Church I usually attend would then be the First Cong. Church here in Oskaloosa, but I do not rely necessarily on this group for my religious guidance.

The Congregational Church as a body have taken no stand on or against military service, however they have recognized and supported their C.O.s and I wish here to stress that my pacifist convictions are on the basis of the society of Friends. From the Society of Friends we have this: We utterly deny war of any form for any pretense whatever,; this is our testimony to the whole world. The spirit of Christ by which we are guided is not changeable, so as to once to command us from a thing of evil, and

141

again to move us into it; and we certainly know and testify to the world that the spirit of Christ, which leads us into all truths, will never move us to fight and war against man with outward weapons, neither for the Kingdom of Christ, nor for the Kingdom of the world.

Therefore, we cannot learn war anymore. And then the later expression; the first contribution our society should make in this period of fear and hate and violence, is a spirit of love and tolerance towards all people, whether they be German, Japanese, Arabs or Jews. It is our fundamental point of view to condemn the war method, whether it be conducted by the dropping of bombs on helpless children or by boycotting helpless women and children, both are equally inhuman and contrary to Friends Principles. (1939)

By November 23, the local draft board contacted Eddy, but this time they sent mail directly to him at college.

Dear sir,

Please furnish this local board affidavits from several people who can verify your position as Conscientious Objector. Please mail prior to December 10, 1948 Bert F. Davis, clerk

Eddy, having been in this position before, had a long list of people he could contact for letters to the draft board, but why they were being requested was unclear. Local Draft Board #121 no doubt had his previous files available to them, but some draft boards took an antagonistic approach toward objectors.

Eddy responded to Board #121:

I would like to take this time to place on file with your office some material which you may deem as pertinent, towards the re-classification of myself. In your letter of Nov.23, 1948 you requested "affidavits from several people who can verify your position as conscientious objector." I have asked several of my friends to write and

142

presume that their letters are in your hands by this date, however it is at this time that I would like to call your attention to several things in my file which may have a bearing on this new situation.

During the first S.S. Act, my classification was refused by the board No.4 Downers Grove and went to appeal. As was the procedure at that time my case was given a study by the Dept of Justice and following that two letters were placed on file, that I would like to quote from. The first is from James F. McGranery, at that time, assistant to the Attorney General, dated December 4, 1944. 'After review of the entire file and record of Everett L. Edwards Jr. The Department of Justice recommends in the above-mentioned case, that the board of appeals, insofar as it concern the question of Conscientious Objections to participation to war, be sustained, and the registrant to be placed in classification 4E and assigned...

The second of these letters is from the Hon. Roy O. West, who was at that time the hearing officer for the Northern District of Illinois. Dated Nov 7, 1944 "since therefore the registrant has both the sincerity and the religious training and beliefs required in order to sustain a claim for exemption as a Conscientious Objector, I conclude that he is entitled to classification as such. Recommendation: I recommend that the

Conscientious Objections of the registrant be sustained and that he be classified in class 4E and in lieu...

I would like to have these two excepts from my last file entered as additional information as to my position as a Conscientious Objector, and also add to this material the fact that on December 10,1946 I received my discharge from "Work of National

Importance under Civilian Direction."

Sincerely, E.L.Edwards Jr.

Eddy received a copy of the letter sent by Eugene

Dungan, Fran's father, on his behalf.

Gentlemen,

I have known Everett L. Edwards Jr. since about 1938-39. He is now a student at William Penn College, Oskaloosa Iowa. My old college, where he is doing important public relations work. His home is at 508 North Grant Street, Hinsdale Illinois.

The Edwards family and mine have been good friends, visiting in each other's homes and meeting in suburban social affairs. As to the religious affiliations the Dungans have been members of the Friends, connected with Friends meetings in Chicago and Oak Park, while the Edwardses have attended the Hinsdale Union Church. Nonetheless our association has been such that I have known this lad's attitudes and beliefs and those of his brother and sister and parents.

The war-time Selective Service law, like the present law, promised exemption from military service to those whose religious belief made it impossible for them to take part in war. Everett Edwards Jr. claimed exemption; he appealed from the boards first decision; and finally had his appeal was granted by the President of the United States on Presidential order he was made a member of Civilian Public Service, where he worked for a good many months.

It seems to me that Everett Edwards Jr. is clearly within the group envisioned by the law makers; a true believer that war for him is forbidden by his Christian belief.

I affirm that the above letter, in all of its statements, is true, to the best of my knowledge and belief.

Respectfully,

Eugene Dungan

On March 1, 1949, Eddy received a re-classification from 1-A to IV-E. For the time being, it appeared that his life had returned to normal.

Chapter 24
On to 1949

While he was writing the U.S. Government, Eddy's involvement with the broadcast department at William Penn increased. He became the executive secretary of the radio program.

He now listed himself as working in public relations. This gave him access to work on the college radio station. At one point, he conducted an on-air interview with Iowa farmer, Art Emory, who had returned from a trip to Europe where he was engaged with a group who were reaching out to not only the farm communities of Germany and other US friendly countries, but also had snuck their way into Russia to speak with groups of farmers there to spread the notion of love and peace for all nations. Eddy recorded the radio broadcast and acted as host, originally recording a much longer interview segment.

Just after the first of the year in 1949, Eddy received news that William Penn college was to host Lowell Thomas for both a lecture and campus broadcast. This was very exciting news for him, and he got off a quick letter to the Thomas camp on official, "Office of the President"
William Penn College stationery.

> Dear Lowell,
>
> Because of my connection with the school broadcasts here at Penn, I have been asked to check with you on arrangements for your visit here. As I understand it, you are to give your lecture here on Friday, January 21. In planning for your broadcasts for that evening, I'd like to place at your disposal our sound studio on the campus. We have a small studio about one-half the size of your

Pawling studio. It is sound-proofed and has a private telephone connection to the central telephone office here in Oskaloosa. The Chapel here on campus, from where the lecture is to be given, also has some sound proofing and has broadcast telephone connection.

If you decide to broadcast from the campus you might have Electra drop me a note on the general time schedule so we may help make advance preparation thus to avoid any possible conflict with your activity. Two thoughts also come to mind along this line of the broadcast. The first: I would like to write the editors of the nearby high school newspapers and invite them to sit in on your 5:45 broadcast. If this would not interfere too much with your plans it would give them a real chance to see a nation-wide broadcast in operation. Ten or fifteen persons would probably be the maximum number involved. Second: For the late evening broadcast you could either go on from the chapel, which would give the audience a chance to see a broadcast—or again, from the studio. Both are on the same private telephone line. Either of these last two thoughts are just suggestions, and are, of course, up to your consent.

Well, that's about all for now and if you could have Electra drop me a line of the high school idea, I could send out invitations. Say "hello" to my friends there and especially John and Barbra. Merry Christmas and Happy New Year!

Sincerely,
Everett Edwards

Eddy had been prophetic when he wrote in his first essay at William Penn: "While at Bowie I started Night school but it was then that I realized that it was going to be hard for me to go back to school."

His activities with the radio station and various music programs began interfering with his general studies. He said as much during a visit with a guidance counselor at the college. He admitted he needed to spend more time on his studies and less time on his extracurricular activities. His grades were suffering as a result.

Once again Eddy had been focusing on the draft, leaving him feeling like he was treading water and a bit adrift. Again, the concept of the draft seemed to derail his life. His time at William Penn was well spent but coming to an unfulfilled conclusion. The spring of 1949 saw the end of Eddy's college experience.

The explosion in the field of consumer electronics captivated him. Were there job opportunities? He didn't know but was determined to find out.

Some of his interest was rooted in his love of folk dancing. He plied his skill as a caller and as a trade and developed a personal square dancing calling style. There was enough opportunity around the Chicagoland area for him to establish himself as a reputable caller.

An idea was born, coming from several directions all at once. What was lacking for the caller was a truly portable way to set up for a dance. Eddy, his father and two others, started their own company: EDDECO Manufacturing. The name was derived from the owners and designers of the company: Edwards/Dungan/Dvorak/Edwards.

They set out to build a unit for calling dances with all the necessary components built in. It all started with a record player turntable. While high-end square dances would have a live band, most required the caller to provide his own source of music. The turntable needed to not only play records at the common speeds, but also needed to have a way to vary the speed, so the caller could speed up or slow down as needed.

Connected to the turntable was all in one amplification, along with a set of housed speakers. The amplifier needed to support its own public address system (PA) with a microphone attached. They envisioned it all being contained in a case that could be carried in one hand, leaving the other hand free to carry their box of records.

Over the past year, Eddy had gained access to a treasure trove of new electronics, which played a part in both his ability to dream about what was needed while acting as a blueprint of sorts, enabling him to envision how the different components might go together to form a new type of machine. Everett Sr., a skilled draftsman, and adept at design, with a large amount of practical building experience. This was a smaller project when compared to buildings he had worked on designing, and certainly smaller than the factory design work he did as an engineer/draftsman. Their other partners brought similar skills to the project.

What ended up standing in the way of EDDECO manufacturing was the extremely small niche market. They only managed to build six units before they dissolved the company.

Even if their record player didn't manage to reach a large audience, the unit they built provided Eddy with a way to help his trade. Following the war, both square dancing and folk dancing had found a foothold as a wholesome social affair. Eddy began to find different avenues for his talent. The Chicago Park District was running folk/square dance programs. Eddy was able to participate by teaching some classes and doing some calling.

On a larger scale, WLS, which was a major player in Chicago AM radio, had a successful radio program called WLS Barn Dance. At the time, it was compared to the Grand Old Opry. This country-music variety show broadcast every Saturday evening from 7-11. Many live music acts and skits performed, but they also had a square dance segment for which, on occasion, they used traveling callers-someone who was not part of their regular cast. Eddy managed to get a gig as a traveling caller and was broadcast on the radio. That may have been the high point of his calling career, for by 1949, the Barn Dance and square dancing began slowly fading in popularity.

One evening, Eddy was going home from an event in the Chicago area. He offered a ride to a young lady whose home was near his Hinsdale residence. On the way to her home, Eddy's beloved '37 Dodge broke down. He had no way to remedy the situation on the road at night, so he left the car on the side of the road. Doing what he felt was right, he escorted the young lady home. After a couple of miles, they arrived at the front gate guarding a long driveway of her home. They used the gate intercom to announce their presence. A car was sent down the driveway, where it picked up the young lady, then drove back up the driveway, offering Eddy no form of assistance or even an offer of a ride back to his car.

The EDDECO record player wasn't Eddy's only venture into modern electronics. By the late 1940's, the first consumer version of the reel-to-reel tape recorder emerged. Eddy had gained experience using tape while at William Penn. He not only learned how to operate the machine, but also learned how to splice the tapes for editing and repairs.[*]

Eddy was fascinated by the expanding commercial market of consumer electronics and obtained a reel-to-reel tape recorder. Though this was very early for home recording, he saw it as a possible way to create extra income. Eddy and Everett Sr. soon found ways to use the recorder.

Eddy had a collection of recordings he did while at William Penn, but those were probably made on the college equipment. He also had a collection of recorded performances of him teaching and calling square dancing.

Everett Sr. used the machine to do family recordings. He did several interviews with elder family members talking and answering questions about family history. Though photography was common, there were almost no family audio records. A small number of home movie cameras were in use, but the addition of audio to the home movies was still years away. In any case, Everett and Eddy saw the potential of this new technology and invested in the equipment.

---

[*] *To splice a tape: the reel-to-reel tape is cut at an angle. Another portion is cut at a similar angle and the two sides are joined together so that when the tape moves over the record or play heads of the recorder, there is a constant stream of tape to record or play.*

They made a few recordings of weddings of friends, showcasing ways to use the machine in hopes of creating a market.

Beside the use of the recorder for people in conversation, there was an obvious use to record live music. On one occasion, Eddy recorded a performance of a good friend of his from Circle Pines, John Sonquest. John was Dave Sonquest's nephew and a highly skilled piano player. On another occasion, they set up for a makeshift recording at the Circle Pines farmhouse for some folk music with Dave Sonquest and a few other musicians playing a variety of stringed instruments.

On one of his later recordings, Eddy recorded Pete Seeger with Big Bill Broozney on guitar for a couple of songs as they hammered out "Talking Atom" (Old Man Atom or Atomic Talking Blues), a Vern Partlow tune, and Talking Union Blues. Pete made several visits to Circle Pines. Big Bill worked there for a few years as a cook.

Eddy and Everett kept finding uses for the recorder. Even Viola got involved, using it to record what was listed as "Viola's first lawsuit," and later sending out congratulations to Ade Robeson for a good try after Robeson lost an election. In later years, Eddy used the recorder to deliver a treasurer's report. (He was Treasurer for Circle Pines at that point) while unable to attend the meeting.

Eddy possessed a knack for being able to see the possibilities of things. A dreamer and schemer, he was a definite idea man. Everett was the proper foil for this. He enjoyed having a project into which he could invest his time and energy. He had done his first home plan drawing at the age of 18 and had spent some time designing and building children's toys.

After receiving the 4-E, Eddy found out that a House Representative had raised an objection to his classification, arguing that because of his discharge, his service with both the U.S. Forest Service and his early release from Civilian Public Service constituted a lack of time served. Though the time in the Forest Service, along with his time at both Camp Wellston and Camp Bowie was considered important public service, and Eddy had no control over when he was discharged, this did not seem to influence the opinion of the Representative. As the battle over his classification continued, life went on.

Bruce was working on his Masters degree. Dorothy had moved away. Everett and Viola and a few other families had purchased a large parcel of land next to Circle Pines with the hope of someday placing a retirement home there. The property was called "the 80" for the 80 acres it occupied.

Everett stayed busy assisting with construction at Circle Pines, lending his ability and expertise as a draftsman architect. Circle Pines was moving forward on the construction of an outdoor pavilion. Everett did the drawing for the massive stone fireplace which occupied one end of the structure. He also got involved with a new co-operative subdivision outside of Chicago called York Center. He worked on drawings, and developed a material takeoff list, cost breakdown and an analysis of structures he had designed, comparing them to similarly designed Frank Lloyd Wright homes.

Eddy, however, was unable to resist the draw of working with children. When a chance to lead a group or to take an outing presented itself, Eddy was the first to volunteer. In the summer of 1949, Eddy took a job at Camp Big Paw, in Watervliet Michigan, on the banks of the Paw Paw River. When he arrived, he was put in charge of the camp's horse program. It was a small program, but Eddy was the only one with any skill at handling the animals. The time he spent at Circle Pines working with their draft horses made him the most qualified.[†]

After the season at Camp Big Paw, Eddy went back to work where he could get it. He was a dreamer, but understood that if a college degree was not in his future, he needed to find ways

---

[†] *It is kind of a camp thing: you don't need to be an expert, you just need to be the most qualified. Since Eddy was the most qualified, the horses became his job.*

to earn a living while educating himself. If a job came along or even a suggestion of a job and it sounded interesting, there was a good chance Eddy was interested.

The gigs with square dance calling had become lucrative enough that Bruce approached Eddy for a loan. Bruce was planning a wedding while finishing up his Masters and was broke. He didn't want to ask Everett and Viola for help, but knew Eddy had been doing quite well with his square dance calling.

While Eddy played many instruments, he was most proficient on the drums. He could knock out a tune or two on piano, but his guitar playing was more for strumming around the campfire. He could have done well as a front man, but didn't see himself as a vocalist or the star of the show. He was fine singing in front of people and with his dance background, could move across a stage with ease. He eyed the possibility of jobs as a side musician with small combos. To acquire the proper gear, he made a trip to downtown Chicago. On Wabash Street, he took an elevator up to the sales floor of Frank's Drum Shop. Both stars and novices frequented the store.

On one memorable trip, he met renowned drummer Louie Bellson there.

Ultimately, however, nothing came of his venture in the world of small band performance. With everything else going on in his life, Eddy struggled with maintaining the discipline for consistent gigging as a member of a group or combo. He ended up gifting the drum set to a family friend for their child who had contracted polio.

On June 27, 1950, one day after Eddy's 24th birthday, the war in Korea broke out. Even with a 4-E classification, he had plenty to be concerned about. For Eddy, there was not only concern for himself, but as someone who had an extremely strong conviction against violence and killing, he worried for the world. He also had to wonder if there would be another change to the draft rules—and if so, how that might affect him.

Chapter 25
The Settlement House

In the spring of 1952, Eddy began to eye his approaching 26th birthday. It may have looked like an arbitrary milestone date, but he was well aware of its significance with his relationship with the draft.

He had settled for a self-employed lifestyle, moving from job to job, without the long term commitments which come with adulthood, but perhaps it was time to look for something more permanent.

Through the years Eddy never lost track of or contact with Fran. They remained close friends. Fran contacted Eddy about a job opening. She had taken a job working on the South Side of Chicago, in the area called "the back of the yards," named for its location in relationship to the stock yards of Chicago—a main source of employment for the immigrant population, which provided plentiful, cheap labor. The job was a for socially conscious organization called the Mary McDowell Settlement House. Fran knew that with Eddy's history and desire to see a better way of running the world, this could be a good match.

Mary McDowell was a prominent Chicago-area force both in politics and social movements. A devout Methodist, McDowell arrived in Chicago in 1870. She worked with the Woman's Christian Temperance Union in the 1880's. She was a kindergarten teacher at Chicago's Hull house, founded the settlement Woman's Club, and in 1894, took charge of a program near the stockyards that the Christian Union of the University of Chicago had started.

Over the next two decades, McDowell secured funding for the University of Chicago Settlement House. She worked to acquire a gymnasium and auditorium and built a three-story building to house the residents and programs.

Serving a population of Irish, German, Bohemian, and Polish families living near the packing houses, the settlement sponsored classes in English and citizenship, and boasted a woman's club, youth groups, a kindergarten, and a playground. Over time, more programs for training "hands on" skills were added for both boys and girls. There were plots of land where small gardens could thrive, and where residents learned how to grow a small amount of food for their own use.

A group of women in the Hyde Park neighborhood, close to the University of Chicago, organized to aid and support the settlement work. With a belief that music is a positive agent in cultural development, the committee secured pianos and made it possible for two settlement residents, aided by volunteers, to organize music classes and teach lessons. Eventually a children's chorus was formed, which grew into a great group of 300 children singing folk songs from their native lands and songs that knew no national boundaries. An adult chorus was added, and soon, artists from all parts of the city began volunteering their services for Sunday concerts.

The settlement house stressed "brotherhoods." McDowell often used the term. However, as with many progressive social movements, there was much mistrust from the politicians who were wary of any reforms. There was a mistrust of ethnic-enclaves and their parish organizations. There was a large amount of mistrust because many of the organizers came from Hyde Park, home of the University of Chicago-many viewed the residents of Hyde Park as snobbish, condescending, middle-class Protestants.

While Mary McDowell stayed true to herself and beliefs, she never stopped working to improve the lives of the less fortunate and the immigrant population of Chicago. The Mary McDowell Settlement House was named in her honor.

The Settlement House movement paralleled much of the history of Circle Pines. This was an organization where Eddy could feel at home. By the early 1950s, much of the settlement population was a mixture of Polish and Hispanic families, mirroring the neighborhoods around the Settlement House—a 180 square block area, from Damen Street on the west, to Morgan Street on the east. From 43rd street to the north, to 51st street to the south. By the time Eddy arrived, the building located at 4655 Gross Ave, which later became McDowell Ave., covered over 45,000 square feet. Much of that was located in a four-story structure which housed club rooms, a library, music room, rooms for manual training and sewing, a nursery to assist the mothers, showers, and a pair of gymnasiums. It served as a central hub of activity for the local area.

Of all the jobs Eddy had worked, Fran was correct in that this looked to be a very good fit. His first job with the Settlement House was to act as chaperone and escort a group of young people from Chicago to Camp Farr in Chesterton, Indiana, about 60 miles away.

Camp Farr was a facility made possible by a donation of $3,000 by University of Chicago alumna Shirley Farr in 1923. It allowed for the purchase of the land, a 40-acre parcel with woods and a creek running through it. The creek provided a natural division of the property into two halves—a farm side and a camp side—with a steep embankment and forest flanking both sides of the creek.

The farm side included the farmhouse, a large two-story red brick home, with stately open porches on two sides painted white to contrast the brick. Looking to the south was the centerpiece of any Indiana farm, a massive post and beam barn with huge double doors twelve feet tall painted red. The barn provided a home for the farm animals and storage for the hay necessary to feed them through the winter. Another outbuilding acted as a cabin for the Wranglers, a working group of young men from the settlement neighborhood. There were a few other assorted outbuildings including a shop constructed of the same red brick as the house. Also, closer to the Wranglers' cabin was a two-seater outhouse with its own oil stove to provide heat.

The camp had its own driveway that crossed a bridge over the creek and wound around to the west side of the campgrounds. By the 1950s, the camp side consisted of a dining hall, six cabins, a craft shop, a full sized swimming pool with shower house, and a large windmill located centrally between the dining hall and swimming pool. A large grassy field separated the gathering area and the cabins. A walking trail through the woods connected the two sides.

The camp took on the Farr family name. Because it was sponsored by the University of Chicago, Camp Farr had an arrangement allowing use of the facility for university programs for a few weeks during the year, as long as they didn't infringe on the summer camp schedule.

Eddy's first group trip for which he served as a chaperone was prior to the Settlement House camp season and was a student school group from the University of Chicago Lab School. This private school opened in 1896 and was named Laboratory School because of a desire to not only be a progressive educational experience, but to also be able to have a forum in which to test ideas on education.

On the tenth of May, 1952, Eddy received a notice of re-classification from 4-E to 1-A from Local Board No.121, Wheaton, IL.

The following day, the notice came to report for his physical.

He was unaware that this was coming. Not once, but twice before, he had already fought for and won the right for a 4-E classification. Of course, he thought that this must be some sort of mistake. But also wondered why, if there was a justification for a reclassification, it had not come back as one of the other classifications for objectors where they could serve in the armed forces, but in a non-combatant capacity.

Eddy knew from his previous experience that there was a chance this was a ploy to get him to ignore proper procedure, and fail to follow through, which would put him at risk for possible incarceration.

He needed to reply right away, so on May 11, the same day he received the letter to report for his physical, he responded to the draft board.

Dear Sirs,

I have received my notice to report for physical examination on May 21, at 9:30 A.M.

I would like to request a postponement of this examination due to my being out of the state on that date. I am joining the staff of the University of Chicago Settlement House, in the back of the yards district of Chicago, and am taking a group of 30 young people to a camp in Indiana for a period of 10 days. As there are only two from the Settlement House going, and the other one must do all the cooking for the group, it would necessitate a great overburdening of an already overburdened staff in order to release someone else to go on such short notice.

I will return to the Chicago area on the 27th of May and as this is only a matter of only seven or eight days, I sincerely hope that this request may be granted.

I am also in receipt of my Notice of Classification. I would like to also request a personal appearance before the board in regards my being reclassified 1-A. The above holds true also in regards to dates for this appearance; anytime after the 27th of May.

Thanking you for your troubles I remain
Sincerely,
Everett Edwards Jr.

Eddy was savvy enough by this point to send this letter certified "return receipt requested."

The letter was delivered to the draft board on May 15, 1952. Containing two separate issues, it required two separate replies from the draft board. Neither came.

Eddy was not about to stay idly still and wait for bad things to happen. He had been schooled well by both Everett Sr. and Viola in how to handle himself in situations like this, and he was not about to let them down. He picked up the phone and called the draft board. There is no recording of the call, (though by this time with all the work he had done with the recorder, he may have told the board the call was being recorded), but the following day he received a telegram from local board 121.

Dear Sir,

Confirming our telephone conversation of May 20, we wish to advise, you will report for physical examination in accordance with SSS Form 223 dated May 9, 1952 to report May 21, 1952. Yours very truly,

FOR THE BOARD

Roceil Magnesen   Acting clerk

Whether it was a late response, an oversight, or perhaps a threat, Eddy didn't know. Only one question had been answered: he was obligated to report for a physical.

This was not how he hoped to kick off a new job. Arrangements needed to be made. He needed to get to the camp after the physical.

He had work to do.

So, on May 21, 1952, Eddy showed up for his physical and was found "fully acceptable for induction into the armed services." The Certificate of Acceptance was signed Orville T. Lowe, Maj.

But there was an additional note on the Certificate: "Any inquiry relative to personal status should be referred to your local board."

Eddy wanted to make sure that he could raise an objection to bearing arms wherever and whenever he could. He wanted his objection legally noticed by the draft board, while the question remained: Why had the board not responded to his request for a hearing? He knew that though there was war in

Korea, the need for manpower via draftees certainly was not at the same level as during WWII. It was a question without an answer, Eddy needed to be patient to see if one would come.

With the physical completed, Eddy drove out to Camp Farr as quickly as he could. It was a new job and he was already late— not an ideal first day. With only two staff members from the Settlement House assigned to this event, he felt the pressure of a possible failure.

There needed to be programs, along with food service for the group of young people, for which he shared responsibility. This was a first glimpse into Eddy's new job, but provided a welcome distraction from his issues with the draft board.

Chapter 26
Camp Farr

Returning to the city after his 10 days in the country, Eddy gathered his belongings and headed back to the camp for the summer session.

He took up residence in the farmhouse and got to know the staff and others who were already living there. There was a farm manager and his wife who oversaw the farm and wintered on site, taking care of the property, a small menagerie of livestock, and a garden program. The garden and farm were an extension of a garden program at the Settlement House, expanded to include live animals. It was used as a teaching tool about how to raise your own food, and with luck, be able to provide some groceries for the camp.

The Settlement House had a program called the Wranglers, consisting of older teenage males from the neighborhood who needed some time away from the city. For some, it was for expanded training, and others, a necessary change of environment. Even though they had their own cabin on the east side of the property, during both the early and late part of the season, the Wranglers would occasionally bunk in the farmhouse.

There were a few weeks before the official start of the summer camp season. Children couldn't come to camp until after schools were officially out for the summer, but there was still plenty of work to do for the first week. Cabins needed to be swept and washed down, and mattresses cleaned. The dining hall needed to be cleaned. The pool house and pool needed to be opened for the season.

In the mad scramble to be ready to open on time, Eddy's biggest fear turned to reality. On June 11, 1952, an "Order to report for induction" from the Selective Service System, was received at his Hinsdale home address. It stated that he was to report at 8:00 A.M. on June 23, 1952, for forwarding to an induction station.

The following note was at the bottom of the form:

> This local board will furnish transportation to the induction station where you will be examined, and if accepted for service, you will then be inducted into a branch of the armed forces.
>
> Persons reporting to the induction station in some instances are found to have developed disqualifying defects since being examined and may be rejected for these or other reasons. It is well to keep this in mind in arranging your affairs, to prevent any undue hardship if you are rejected at the induction station. If you are employed, you should advise your employer of this notice and the possibility that you may not be accepted at the induction station. Your employer can then be prepared to replace you if you are accepted, or to continue your employment if you are rejected.
>
> If you are not accepted, return transportation will be provided.
>
> Willful failure to report promptly to this Local Board at the place specified above and the hour and day named in this notice is a violation of the Selective Service Act of 1948 and subjects the violator to fine and imprisonment.
>
> You must keep this form and bring it with you when you report to the Local Board. Bring with you sufficient clothing for 3 days.

Eddy was not able to make any sense of this level of incompetence from Local Board 121, Wheaton, Illinois. While the notice went to Hinsdale, either he returned to Hinsdale to retrieve the letter, or the letter was brought to him by Everett Sr.

On June 14, 1952, Eddy responded to the Local Board No. 121:

Dear Sirs,

On the tenth of May of this year, I received a "notice of Classification" from your board stating that I had been re-classified 1-A. The following day I received a "Notice to report for a physical". A letter was sent to you the following day in regard to both the physical and the re-classification. I am now in receipt of my "Order to report for induction" for the 23rd of June.

On the left hand margin of your Notice of classification (form 110) it says "Within the same 10 day period you may file a written request for personal appearance before the local board. If this is done, the time in which you may appeal is extended to 10 days from the mailing of the new notice of classification, after such a personal appearance."

The fourth paragraph of my letter to you on May 11, 1952, reads, "I am also in receipt of my notice of classification. I would like also to request a personal appearance before the local board in regards my being reclassified 1-A". To date I have received no word from you in regard to this hearing. Does this mean that I am to be deprived of my appeal? I certainly wish to place my appeal on file with your board., but according to your own directives this would come after the question of a personal appearance or board reconsideration was taken care of. If the hearing is still pending, or the appeal, then what is the status of the order to report?

Since 1945 I have had the classification of 4-E or a conscientious objector. This classification was obtained from the Presidential Appeal Board during the early part of that year. Since the old classification of 4-E has been replaced by the new 1-O I would hope that you would see your way clear to classify me as such.

Please address all correspondence to me at Camp Farr, Chesterton, Indiana.

Sincerely, Everett Edwards

A new game began for Eddy—Waiting for a telegram or letter which likely would not come.

Eddy was well aware that three days after he was to be inducted into the Armed Forces, on June 26, he would turn 26. He was also aware that the Selective Service Act of 1948 made him draft eligible until his 26th birthday.

It wasn't certain whether the game the draft board was playing was to try to induct him before his birthday, or if the Board members who disapproved of Conscientious Objectors expected him to make an error in his duty to report, and make him eligible for arrest.

Eddy wasted no time and quickly got off a letter to the National Service Board of Religious Objectors on June 17:

Hi Gang,

Never thought I'd be dropping you a line again as the last time you looked at my file must have been 1944 or 5. Here is the latest thing of whirl-wind courtships with the draft board I've seen yet. It starts with a notice of classification on the May 11th and end with an induction refusal on the 23rd of this month. (This letter not yet sent-only word from them would hold it up) They have said nothing at all about a personal appearance and in doing so deprived me of my right to appeal.

The fact that I will be 26 on the 26th of June undoubtably has something to do with it, yet it really seems to make an interesting case. Thought that you might like to see it, I will let you know how things progress. Thanks for all your past help,

Everett L. Edwards Jr.

Eddy had a job to do and a camp to open. His plan was to stay focused and charge straight ahead.

With the following doomsday letter written, he placed it in an envelope marked "don't mail."

Dear Sirs,

I have received my "Order to Report for Induction"

for the 23rd of June. This is to notify you that I will not appear for said induction. I have tried in every way possible to co-operate with your office in order to follow through the legal channels to the obtaining of classification as a conscientious objector.

Since my classification as such from the Presidential appeal board in 1945, to the present date I have been classified this way. Once before I have been reclassified 1-A, only to have it changed upon appeal.

On the tenth of May this year I received Notice of re-classification. On the eleventh of May I received a notice to report for a physical. On the eleventh of May I requested a personal appearance before your board. On the 23 of May I received my physical examination, the paper of which were marked "Conscientious Objector". On June 11th you mailed an "Order for Induction" for the 23rd of June. Nowhere yet have I been allowed to appear for my hearing, nowhere yet has my case been reconsidered, nor have I yet been allowed to place an appeal with the appeal board. I still fail to comprehend just how the Induction Notice could have been sent out.

Yet—this notice is here; I have no alternative but to refuse the notice. I will remain here at Camp Farr till I hear from you or from the Justice Dept.

Sincerely, Everett L. Edwards Jr.

Chapter 27
June 23, 1952

There is some confusion over what exactly happened next, or why.

Eddy received a telegram from Local Board No. 121. The stamp indicating the official date on the top of the page was stamped June 2? something, which was obscured by a handwritten "17" over it.

The date on the text read June 17, 1952. From a note on the bottom:

cc: Col. Paul C Armstrong, State Director.

Dear Sir,

This local board is postponing your Induction on June 23, 1952 in accordance with Section 1632.2 of the Selective Service Regulations. Your case will be reviewed at the next Local Board meeting.

Yours very truly,

FOR THE BOARD

Roceil Magneson   Acting clerk

Eddy was spared sending his letter. Because the date had been changed on the document, and since Eddy's letter was not mailed on Saturday the 21st of June, the telegram arrived either on June 20 or 21.

By Tuesday, June 24, he was met with another telegram:

Dear Sir,

In accordance with Selective Service Regulations, your order to Report for

Induction, June 23, 1952, is hereby cancelled by authority of the State Director.

Yours very truly,

FOR THE BOARD
Roceil Magnesen   Acting clerk

Two days later, Eddy turned 26. At no point since the start of his journey with the Selective Service, had he had this sense of freedom.

The summer happened way too fast. Eddy threw himself into his work. He loved the work with kids and the job felt almost magical to him. Whether it was as the lifeguard yelling, "K-P out of the pool"* a half hour before mealtime, or the time spent leading group singing around the campfires at night, he could allow himself to be happy.

He was a bit of an outsider, a white, Protestant suburbanite, but it mattered not. The families of the Settlement House, while for the most part Polish, Mexican and Catholic, had for years blended their families as the different groups came together with one goal—to be good Americans. To the credit of the Edwards family and the influence of the years at Circle Pines, Eddy had no preconceived notions or prejudices. His exposures to all walks of life, religions, and races had left him with this philosophy: "Family is not defined by blood, family is defined by who you love and who loves you back."

The job with the Settlement House lasted past the summer of 1952, as he slowly lost the need to look over his shoulder for the next battle with Selective Service.

As fall came, Eddy was part of the staff and had taken up residence at the Settlement House in Chicago. He worked in the game room, helping to organize and run all the different events and programs in the house.

In 1953, a new director was hired. Dan DeFalco was a likable man with a background in social work. That same year, the property manager at Camp Farr departed, leaving an opening for someone to take over the full-time position at the

---

* K-P is short for "kitchen patrol"—those who needed to report to the dining hall to set up for the upcoming meal.

camp. Eddy jumped at the chance. He moved out to Camp Farr as the full-time resident facility manager or director. He was still involved with Circle Pines, and was serving on their board of directors, but this felt right for him.

Eddy lived in the brick farmhouse and assumed the responsibility of the animal care. During the summer months the house also played host to Dan DeFalco and his family as Dan came to camp to act as director of the summer programs.

As on-site director, Eddy needed to take charge of work programs to ensure the camp maintenance was being done. The Wranglers were under his control. This group of testosterone fueled young men was a challenge. With his background of non-violence as a Quaker, Eddy provided a barrier for them they had not come across before.

With a large in-ground pool on site, Eddy found a use for his diving gear he acquired at Quaker Hills. The dive mask allowed him to inspect various parts of the pool while it was filled with water.

The whole process was a foreign concept for the Wranglers. At least one of the boys thought it would be funny to turn off the compressor supplying Eddy with air while he was underwater. Eddy shot to the surface spitting mad. When he found out what had happened, even as a joke, he had to contain himself. (In the Wranglers' defense, they claimed it was done as a work protest and that after the incident, their workload was more balanced.)

While for the most part Eddy was able to control the situation peaceably, a clash was bound to happen.

In another instance, one of the Wranglers accosted Eddy from behind and put him into a choke hold. Eddy, not knowing what was happening, maneuvered very quickly, flipping his assailant over his head and onto the young man's back. He was very familiar with such a move— he used it in the water as a way to gain control of a drowning victim who was fighting with his rescuer.

This did not set well.

The Wrangler got up embarrassed and threw down a challenge at Eddy.

Not having grown up in the same environment as these young men, Eddy was unaccustomed to what that meant. Evidently, when you grow up in the shadow of street gangs, as so many of these men had, a challenge is a serious action, with hard set rules and consequences.

In accepting the challenge, Eddy had agreed to a situation he knew little about.

An elder Wrangler spoke up. He pointed out that a challenge was given, and the challenge was accepted, but as the one who was challenged, Eddy had the option of choosing the weapons and location.

Eddy grinned.

"That's easy, Open hands in the deep end of the pool."

Eddy's challenger looked crestfallen.

His reply, "But I don't know how to swim."

Though things could have ended badly, the challenge became a bonding moment between Eddy and the Wranglers. He had earned his stripes with them, gaining a level of respect he couldn't command them to give him. In many respects, this was Eddy's new adopted family.

Since the age of 16, Eddy lacked a permanent home. By the summer of 1953, he had been with the Settlement House a full year—the longest he had held a job since his paper route. He had a job that he liked and, perhaps, a sense of peace.

There was still a missing part of his life. Even though Fran and Eddy were very close, their relationship had moved away from boyfriend-girlfriend bonding. Perhaps while fighting for his convictions, Eddy could not see himself involved in a committed relationship, but during the previous year, he had seen his life evolve into something completely different. Fran, while allowing Eddy the space he needed to grow, always held a desire that they would end up together. She was heartbroken that it didn't happen.

In August of 1953, the Settlement House held a week-long "Mothers Camp" for mothers with young children. During the camp, Eddy met and became attracted to Stella, a young widow with a young son in tow.

Stella, although she didn't find Eddy very stylish or attractive, thought his looks were ok. Dressed in his blue jeans with a tucked in white tee shirt, she was taken by how he was unlike any of the men she had met before.

During one evening, Eddy became engaged in a game of spoons† with a group of the mothers, including Stella, who became more and more attracted to him as the game progressed.

Following the game, Eddy and Stella spent some quiet moments talking on a grassy hill in the shadow of the swimming pool fence. They discovered that their dreams and life goals were the same. They shared a common desire for a family, with similar thoughts about how they saw their future. One night turned into many.

They moved quickly from a mutual attraction to a fast-moving romance.

Eddy proposed to Stella in the early fall of 1953, with "I can't promise you wealth or riches, but I can promise you a life more interesting than you can imagine."

They married on October 13, 1953, with Stella, the city girl, and her son moving to the country and Camp Farr, where a new life awaited them all.

---

† *In the game of spoons, players try to collect four of a kind by passing a card around the table. When four of a kind is achieved, that player grabs a spoon from the center of table. A player who does not get a spoon, instead gets a letter. When your letters spell spoon, you are eliminated from the game.*

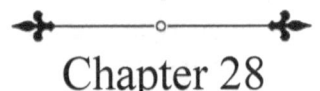

Chapter 28

Biography written by Everett "Eddy" Edwards 9/1947
It's been fun so far

One of the hardest things in my life to do is write an auto-biography that is not too long. Twenty-one years is a long time for things to happen in and I find my life is no exception to the rule. To the contrary, however, I find that so far I have had an exciting and to me, thrilling life, and from all the signs there is much more ahead. As you proceed through these next few pages you will naturally find that I have left out much material, most of which comes in two classifications. These are a book in themselves.

In order to start this out at the beginning I must give you a little of my background. I was born June twenty-six (26) in a small community in suburban Chicago, called Hinsdale. Hinsdale Illinois had at that time, nineteen Twenty six (1926) a population of about Five thousand five hundred (5,500) people. Built on top of an old hill it ran on down to and old historic grist mill on the first corduroy road west of Chicago. Hinsdale was a slow growing community and had its wealthy section although no realy poor section. It had just purchased a new power and water plant, and was justly proud of itself when I came into the picture.

Ma and Pa Edwards were a young couple that had just moved into Hinsdale and settled if you called it that. They had just bought a part of a farm on the edge of town, designed their own home, built it partially theirselves, did their own electrical work and then Me. At the time I was born there were already two young members of this family. My sister Dorothy, five, and my brother, Bruce, two. The folks had very definite ideas on how a family should run and proceeded on their plan to carry these through according to plan.

At the tender age of five I entered that large brick building called the schoolhouse.

Monroe school was only six and one-half blocks from our house and so I could easily walk to and from it every day, cutting across the play field and the park. I shall attempt to speed this up by classifying all my grade school together.

I found early in school that I had a liking for music and so at seven started taking drum lessons. I also had a desire to build things and a great love for the out of doors. I would never tire of playing outside and spent many hours down at my favoritejunk yard swinging from tree to tree on a vine or a rope that we would string up. This of course came later in fifth or sixth grade. We flew kites and went walking to the old mill or along the creek. We spent hours in the woods or on the hills. In the winter you would find us, (Webb Anderson, my buddy) sledding, skating bob sledding and whatever else you can do in the winter time.

Scholastically we did about an average of "C" Not good; not bad. Neither of the two of us were much interested in the grades we got and so didn't really apply ourselves. We liked art, music and best of all recess.

Nineteen thirty-nine (1939) I was at least twelve and already for a move to Junior high School, also about six blocks from our home. Here I became acquainted with many new people from the other grade schools and all of the old friends from Monroe. The studies were much harder but much more interesting. The teachers as a whole were nice but before long I ran into a Miss Cline with whom I have been on uneasy terms ever since. You will hear more about her later on. Miss Cline taught History and Social Studies and once you received a grade from her you carried that on all through school.

I went out for cheerleading and a few sports that year including tumbling. It was during this that I hurt my back and gained the fear of going over backwards, and that has bothered

171

me ever since. I was a cheerleader that year and earned a letter for that and one for intramural football. It was while I was in Junior High School that I began to drift from my friends in Hinsdale and started going with a group from the neighboring towns, in a different type of organization. During the summer of Nineteen thirty-seven to thirty-nine I had been attending with my folks, a Co-operative summer camp in Michigan. Here we learned swimming, diving, leather craft, wood craft, and best of all folk and square dancing. When we were home I ran around with the same bunch of young people from camp, formed a club, had interesting discussions and danced the dances of many lands.

Nineteen forty saw me entering those doors of secondary education n called High School.

Moving into a new building, more classrooms, more students and a more concentrated program, I looked over my studies. English, Social Studies, Speech, Band, Drawing,-Not bad. A very good band and another Cline for Social Studies, but otherwise alright.

Recreation found me in the band room practicing, square dancing or hiking. Old friends and new ones kept me going. Not much really happened that year except getting adjusted. One more year found me a sophomore and studying Biology, English, Band, Drawing, and once again Nellie Cline for American History. This year several things began to happen. I had to defend my pacifist viewpoints continually, I had an older group I ran around with which meant that I didn't need the High School bunch. I was interested in starting a discussion club during lunch period for those who wanted to and was begun to be considered a radical in a group of conservatives and personally felt slightly ill at ease with the old friends. I still studied moderately hard and received average grades.

The junior year at Hinsdale High is one that I cannot easily describe. It was very fast in passing, yet it was not till then that, should I say 'the top blew off'? The key person responsible for all the bickering at school that year was the Principal H. Mossman. Mossman was a very one tracked person with, in my opinion, very little fore-sight. He proceeded, as soon as he took over the position the year before, to insist on his approval that the student council did. This of course had drastic effects on the student body, more of which we shall hear about later. My personal trouble started innocently enough by a friend of mine and myself comparing the grades we had received during the last four years only to find a very unusual fact. Our grades from the Cline sisters had been the same for four and a half years, and it didn't seem right. After checking this fact with others in the class we found the same to be true in most on the other cases in the class. For a six week period, three of us turned in no assignments and flunked the exam, and yet no change. The next six week period saw us handing in excellent papers (with the help of others), got excellent grades on our exams and still no grade change. With these papers behind us and with over sixty percent of the class showing no grade change in four years we went to the principal and pointed this fact to him, wherein he promptly told us that it was none of our business.

Not very long later a student was discharged and the student body struck in protest. Hearing about the walk out in advance the principal locked the doors, which almost disastrous when the fire alarm rang. Although I was not one of the group that planned this strike I was called up before the principal and questioned about the incident. Even to this day I cannot realize the reason that he was allowed the run of that school as long as he was. Things were about to pop at school and we jumped first. In protest to his control, the students disbanded the Student Council with the approval of their advisors. He counteracted by firing nine teachers as of the end of the school year. Band, Art, English, Drama were all losing the heads of their department. The last thing that our English teacher did was to have all her English classes hand in essays on democracy in the schools. It was not long before I discovered that Mossman had read mine.

Big things happened that summer that changed the entire plans that I had made. During the summer at our Co-op summer camp it was decided that they would keep the farm open all winter and that a group of high school students would live there and go to school there. It took only one look at the new school to decide that it was the school for me. I went back to Hinsdale immediately to prepare things and on the way home we stopped in at the high school to get my transfer made out, only to discover, much to our surprise that they had already been made out leaving only the name of the new school out. We had little choice.

My Senior year at Middleville was wonderful. Thirteen miles each way to school and a bus, up early, cold rooms, rough and wild. Very nice teachers and students, very progressive, and an entirely different philosophy and approach. There were seven of us that year and we all had a wonderful time.

Here we have covered to a fair degree the highlights in my schooling a few things happened coincidental to these things. We have seen a radical element moving into me and a tendency towards negative personality. All through High School at Hinsdale I worked for my spending money. I carried papers from five to seven every morning for the first two years and from four till seven thirty during my Junior year. I had become increasingly interested in open discussion groups and my recreation still consisted of non-competitive sports. I was keenly interested in world events and Co-ops and as we shall soon see the Selective Service system. The same year that I graduated from Middleville Michigan, I became that dreaded age of eighteen. I registered at the draft board and filled out form forty-seven for religious objectors. From June that year till Sept one I was a life guard at our camp. From there I went back to newspapers from three to nine every morning. This I kept up till December when my doctor advised me to change hours and climate. A few days later found me aboard the Santa-

Fe Chief as third chef. After working twenty hour shifts, dead tired and very sick I stayed with some friends for several days. Having total assets of only six dollars in my pocket I decided that I had better hit the trail and left Los Angeles via the thumb. Seven days later I arrived home after hitch hiking three thousand miles, visiting Mexico and major cities along the way. I also had gotten rid of all of my nervousness so felt very good.

Ehen I returned home from California I headed into the loop in Chicago to see some old friends of mine at National Co-operatives and got a job right then and there, as an office boy. The job fitted me wonderfully and I stayed there till I was drafted.

Here in the last year I had gathered much valuable material. I had traveled more, worked at different types of work and met many new kinds of people. I had become interested in the American Friends Service Committee, and other organizations and was living a fast tempo and yet had complete freedom.

June twenty, Nineteen forty-five I was drafted into Civilian Public? Service. The first camp I entered was Camp Wellston in the hills of Michigan. It was here that I really began to learn things. In our classed, open discussion and many other places I got a type of education that was not taught in the schools. Cooking at the camp I had time to work outside between shifts and so was able to keep up some spending money. I had been there only three months, however that I was chosen among six to go on an experiment for the Forest Service. The story of this is a book in itself and I cannot handle it now. The extent of the project covered these states; Mississippi, Louisiana, Arkansas, Texas, Oklahoma, Alabama, Florida, and Georgia. These were the main states that we worked in. All the time getting to know the people and their problems. Also getting to love more and more the out of doors.

Returning to Wellston January second I was put on a research project till the close of camp when I was transferred to Camp Bowie, Md. Camp Bowie is another matter I won't

175

go into. It was a sore spot for everyone involved. Rotten food, poor administration, few facilities, small staff all put together means a continuous struggle.

Looking over my time in C.P.S., I found that I had accomplished two major things. One, I had learned many different types of wok and learned new skills. Second, I had increased my fund of knowledge many fold including a terrific course in comparative religions. While at Bowie I started in night school but it was then I realized that it was going to be hard for me to go back to school.

December , 'Fourty-six saw me with my discharge papers in my hands and home for Christmas. I went back to the National Co-operative for work again and this time into the accounting dept. I made an attempt at school again and because of work couldn't keep it up. It was during my return from C.P.S. that I was doing educational work with a Co-operative high school age youth group. This took up a great deal of my time and this added to other conferences and committees speeded me up more than ever. At the beginning of summer there came an opening at our office and so I transferred to Purchasing Office supplies.

I mentioned a brother and a sister on my first page. Dorothy is six years older than I am. She went to the same schools except not in Michigan, all "A" student. Blackburn College and then two years at the U. of Wisconsin. Also "A" From her graduation she went to work for various places and finally for the Chicago offices of the A.F.S.C. till she married Bernard Aldrich, an ex Pennite.

Bruce is my senior two years. After High school he enrolled at Kalamazoo College in that town. After two years his case came up for the federal before the Federal Judge and he was sentenced to three years in the penitentiary for draft evasion. (I might add here that he was refused his four-E classification even though he was majoring in religion.) After seven months in prison he was paroled to the hospital at the University of Michigan. He stayed there a while, jumped paroll went to New

Windsor, Cattleboat for three trips and then back to Uni. Of Michigan where he is now studying.

Having a boy in a major University is a great expense for a family and on top of that we have a grandmother living with us who is semi-invalid and requires a full time nurse. I was not till a few weeks ago that a change in fathers job made it possible to come to Penn. I came here, instantly liked it, took among other courses orientation and had to write an autobiography and here it is.

You will notice that I have left out three major fields of thought in this writing. Each one of these should be handled as a supplement as they are a story in themselves. One is, as you may have noticed, no girlfriends. The second is a very important one and that is my church life. I am a Congregational and Chairman of the local missionary action committee for three years. The third classification is the one I feel I should do at a later date and that is our family. We have always had fun together and have developed a philosophy that nis very easy to follow and that everyone appreciated equally well. If you would like these I will be willing to add them at a later date.

September 14, 1947

Everett L. Edwards Jr.

Deep end of the pool-the genesis of a story

A simple job, much work, but simple. Clean out a third-floor attic.

Sometime in the early 2000s, we were due for our bi-annual fire inspection at our family's summer camp. Inspections are never fun, and I generally dread them, that year was no exception.

I had a good working relationship with our inspector having worked with him for over a decade, but this year was different. I took note when he emerged from his car that his body language and demeanor was different from previous years. I quickly found out that he had been engaged in several administration fights over the last few weeks and was to put it bluntly, in a bad mood. This inspection was not going to go well.

During a walk-through of the dining hall, he noticed and then inquired about a locked door. A door which leads to the attic of the building, a door which during an inspection years earlier, he told me to put a padlock on the door and that would suffice, because after all it just leads to the attic and a non-camper occupied area.

The dining hall is a large building which was previously used as a church and sat at the corner of the property. Early 1900s, the church was disbanded, and the building reverted to the property owner who decided it better served his purpose if it sat down at his farm, a quarter of a mile away.

With teams of horses and logs for rollers, they moved the massive building down the road, set it on a new foundation and converted it into a cow barn, with the cows in the basement, and hay and grain storage on the floors above, where the sanctuary had been.

When we purchased the property in 1964, outlines of pews were still visible on the wainscoting of a room twenty-five feet by twenty-five feet with an eleven-foot ceiling. The attic area spanned over that room and the rest of the building for a total of 1250 square feet of storage with fourteen feet of clearance to the peak above.

That is a large amount of empty space. At one point it served as a radio shack, with work benches and electronics, but mostly, it was just raw storage shared with occasional bats. It was a place for boxes of paperwork, old furniture, extra kitchen equipment and all manner of the excess that accumulates through years of staying in one place. There were two sets of shelves that had been saved from a local mercantile store dating back to the early 1900's. Nine feet high and two feet wide, they stretched eighteen feet across the space, completely filled, along with piles of boxes lining the floor.

All had to be removed to pass the inspection.

It was a task I had to oversee and guide. I found assistance to bring the boxes down from the attic, however, the boxes contained the history of the family business along with the remnant of long-gone hobbies, and projects. Sorting was a project only a family member could handle.

There had been several family businesses in addition to the camp. Dad had a real estate business, along with a few failed ventures. There were files from our days at Camp Farr that moved with us from Indiana to Michigan. There were boxes from my grandparents' estate with part of their history. In the end, every box needed to be sorted. Every sheet of paper was examined, and a decision about its final resting place decided. Most ended up in the fire barrel.

Unable to predict my own future, I now believe I threw away many treasures, items I would now keep. I was unable to see what future projects I might undertake. There was one file folder I found in a box of real estate forms that caught my eye.

179

It was a folder of correspondence between my father and the Selective Service about his quest to become a Conscientious Objector. I set the folder aside, and later moved it to my truck. At the very least, I thought it could be an interesting read for the family. It was something to keep until I could get around to making copies from everyone.

It moved to a drawer in my desk where it sat for many years.

My sister, Sally, made copies of a biography our father had written during his first year in college and passed it out to all the siblings. Reading through the biography and remembering the file in my desk drawer, I began to think there was a compelling story here. I reached out to a friend-client of mine who is a writer, I inquired about how an idea moves from an idea to a written story. Her suggestion was this is something I could write. She could provide me with the framework and mentor me through the process. I let that scary thought sit for a few months.

When I decided to try and take on this project, my only expectation was to end up with something I could share with family, but as I worked through the research, and began the layout, the story became much bigger and more in depth than I imagined.

The process by which you examine your family history and stare at what you know of your parents and their life growing up is both terrifying and revealing. My process began to reveal truths about my father, not in a negative way but I began to understand the man in a new and different way. A whole new way for me to admire who he was. It's a story I now wish to share with both those who knew him and those who didn't.

Acknowledgements

This is a page to pay tribute to those who helped me make this book possible.

First and most certainly foremost was Ami Hendrickson, author, and book coach. If not for her both at beginning encouraging me to take this leap into writing, but for providing me a how-to instruction guide and then acting as mentor along the way. Without her none of this happens.

Christyl Burnett, both as a writer and archivist I leaned on Christyl's knowledge about the history of Circle Pines and she help me gain access to old camp files.

The archivist at Swarthmore College, Anne Yoder, who helped me track down the American Friends Service Committee files for both Eddy and Bruce.

The archivist at Marist College, John Ansley, who tracked down information about Eddy's time at Quaker Lakes Estate and correspondence with Lowell Thomas.

John Brockway, and the Pawling Historical Society and Derek Brockhoff, Historian at Quaker Hills Country Club who helped me fill in some gaps about Eddy's time at Quacker Hills.

The Center on Conscience and War.org and Maria Santelli and Bill Gavin who helped direct me to the archives from the American Friends Service Committee.

Eric and Catherine Sonquist for taking the time to help me with information on their uncle, Dave Sonquist.

Melissa Mendez for supplying me with insight into her mother Fran Dugan, and information about the relationship between Eddy and Fran.

The alumni of both Mary McDowell Settlement House and Camp Farr and the alumni of Circle Pines. All were quick to share stories about the Edwards family.

Plus, a shout out to sisters Amy and Sally who helped remind me of family stories I forgot along the way.

About the Author

Dave Edwards is a drummer, builder, designer, maker of things, martial artist, father, husband, song writer, and brewer. He has followed many paths of interest while raising his family, rebuilding an old farmhouse, performing with his band, seeing to the needs of the family's summer camp and stable business while running a construction business in rural Michigan.

Born and raised in rural Indiana, and moving to Michigan when he was nine, Dave accepted the gift of knowledge from both parents, becoming skilled with his hands, working in the family business of summer camps, and learning how to manage a small business. His mother's passion to become a writer intrigued him and he tried to support her dream, but it wasn't until recently that his venture into writing was more than a short story or letter writing. He became fully engaged in putting together his father's story, realizing that the stories we tell our children are perhaps not the only ones we should share.

www.ingramcontent.com/pod-product-compliance
Lightning Source LLC
Chambersburg PA
CBHW030251130626
46549CB00002B/482